Globalization in Rural Mexico

Globalization in Rural Mexico

Three Decades of Change

FRANCES ABRAHAMER ROTHSTEIN

University of Texas Press ◆ *Austin*

Excerpts from Chapters 4 and 5 were published under the title Flexibility for whom: Small-scale garment manufacturing in rural Mexico, in *Petty capitalists and globalization: Flexibility, entrepreneurship, and economic development,* ed. Alan and Josephine Smart. Albany, NY: State University of New York Press, 2004.

Some material in Chapter 6 was previously published in Frances Abrahamer Rothstein, Challenging consumption theory: Production and consumption in Central Mexico, in *Critique of Anthropology* 25(3) and is reproduced by permission of Sage Publications Ltd. (Copyright Sage Publications, 2005).

Requests for permission to reproduce material from this work should be sent to:
    Permissions
    University of Texas Press
    P.O. Box 7819
    Austin, TX 78713-7819
    www.utexas.edu/utpress/about/bpermission.html
⊗The paper used in this book meets the minimum requirements of ANSI/ NISO Z39.48-1992 (R1997) (Permanence of Paper).

Library of Congress Cataloging-in-Publication Data

Rothstein, Frances.
    Globalization in rural Mexico : three decades of change / Frances Abrahamer Rothstein. — 1st ed.
        p.   cm.
    Includes bibliographical references and index.
    ISBN-13: 978-0-292-71631-5 (cloth : alk. paper)
    ISBN-10: 0-292-71631-1 (cloth : alk. paper)
    ISBN-13: 978-0-292-71632-2 (pbk. : alk. paper)
    ISBN-10: 0-292-71632-X (pbk. : alk. paper)
    1. Mazatecochco (Mexico)—Economic conditions.   2. Mazatecochco (Mexico)—Social conditions.   3. Clothing trade—Mexico—Mazatecochco.
4. Globalization—Mexico—Mazatecochco. I. Title.
    HC138.M33R667   2007
    303.48′27247—dc22

                                                                          2006023443

For the women, men, and children of San Cosme Mazatecochco

Contents

Acknowledgments

This book owes its greatest debt to the people of San Cosme who have shared their time, lives, homes, and knowledge with me for more than thirty years. Without their kindness, generosity, and thoughtfulness, this book could never have been written. A number of families have been especially helpful—time and time again. The Xicohténcatl Rojas family has welcomed me, my husband, and my son into their household on repeated visits. Hilda Corte Mena has been the friend and mentor who always knew what I needed—whether it was work-related or personal—often even before I did. Marcos Xicohténcatl Rojas, in addition to welcoming us into his home, has been an invaluable source of information about the textile industry and work in general. Their son and daughters (Jaime, Silvia, and Laura) and grandson Fabian and his wife, Jenny Xicohténcatl Carmona, have worked as very capable and helpful research assistants. Elvia, Gloria, and Hector have been warmhearted friends as well as very knowledgeable and sensitive observers.

The Mena Sanchez family have also always been very hospitable friends and informative guides. I am grateful to Caratina Perales Lara and the late Florentino Mena Sanchez, especially for the long walks to the mountain and their lessons about agriculture. The Xicohténcatl Sanchez family, the Flores family, especially Candida Flores Cortes, and the Xicohténcatl Ramirez family, especially Cecilia, Olivia, and Joel, have taught me over the years about various aspects of life in San Cosme, ranging from politics, kinship, education, work and garment production to marriage and other important life cycle events. Sofia Mena Sanchez, a teacher and former president of the community, facilitated my initial arrival in the community, invited me to stay with her, and provided a unique understanding of the community and its regional context.

Juan Perales Xicohténcatl, the municipal president in 2005, facilitated my research and provided a very warm welcome to my colleagues from Maryland. I am particularly grateful also to Desiderio H. Xochitiotzin, who introduced me to San Cosme and whose combined historian's and artist's perspective helped me to appreciate Tlaxcala. To the many others whom I have not mentioned and who have welcomed me and my family and who have made the trips to San Cosme not only a very rewarding intellectual experience but a very meaningful part of our lives forever, thank you very much. I thank also the Department of Social and Political Sciences and the graduate students in my class on globalization at the Universidad Iberoamericana for their warm welcome and valuable suggestions. Special thanks to Carmen Bueno Castellano and David Robichaux for their continued encouragement and for helping me become affiliated with Universidad Iberoamericana during the fall of 2001.

A number of people in the United States have also provided valuable advice and suggestions. I am especially grateful to Barbara Leons, who has been not only a great teacher and colleague but also a longtime and dear friend who carefully read and provided helpful criticism on an earlier version of this book. The members of the Women and Work Group, Chris Bose, Myra Marx Ferree, and Carole Turbin, read and discussed many of the papers on which this book is based and encouraged me to put it all together in a single book. Other scholars who have offered valuable comments on earlier interpretations and analyses include Eva Friedlander, Hanna Lessinger, Setha Low, June Nash, Barbara Price, Gloria Rudolf, and Alan Smart. Jayne French entered the data for the quantitative analysis and provided invaluable assistance on numerous tasks.

Generous grants from Towson University, the National Endowment for the Humanities, the Fulbright Foundation, and the Wenner-Gren Foundation for Anthropological Research supported various phases of the research.

Finally, I thank Bob and Jonathan for helping me to get through the hard parts of this journey and for enjoying the research and life in San Cosme so much.

Globalization in Rural Mexico

CHAPTER 1

Introduction: Anthropology and Globalization

When I first went to San Cosme Mazatecochco, a rural community in the state of Tlaxcala in central Mexico, in 1971, there were only a few small stores, and they sold just some fruits and vegetables, canned sardines, cigarettes, soda, beer, and candy. A few daily buses traveled the unpaved main street to a nearby highway and then on to the city of Puebla about ten miles away. Today, hundreds of the town's residents own cars, buses, and taxis, and *convis* (minivans) travel the many paved streets and the new highway that run through the community. Numerous stores in San Cosme now sell just about anything, including Internet access.

When friends, acquaintances, students, or colleagues hear about these and other changes, they usually respond with satisfaction that San Cosme is now sharing the benefits of modernization. But then, after a few minutes, they often question me as to whether such changes are really beneficial or whether the community has lost something in the process. My inclination, especially because I know that much of this modernization is related to the huge growth of garment workshops (which can be likened to sweatshops[1]), is to judge the changes more harshly. My first response is concern about the costs of the contemporary life-style. Although many people can now buy an array of goods never before available to them, most are working harder and longer than ever. When I stop to consider what people in San Cosme say, however, I must recognize that they, like so many others, are pleased that they are now sharing at least some of the benefits of modernization.

This book speaks of and to the contradictions and complexities of modernization in San Cosme and by extension to communities elsewhere in the developing world. What are their gains and losses? Who has gained? And who has lost? San Cosme has been modernizing for

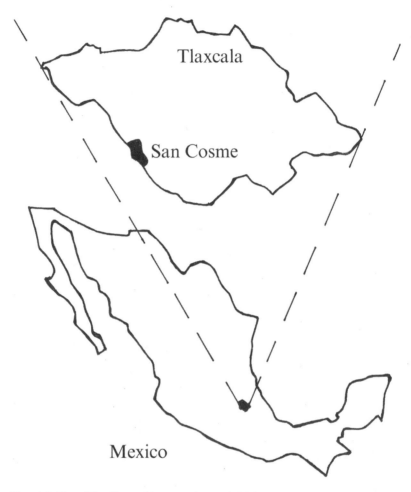

Map 1.1. Map of San Cosme Mazatecochco and vicinity

some time. My earlier research described the shift from family agriculture to factory wage work as the primary source of income in the post–
World War II period. Proletarianization, increased concern with education, and infrastructural change, including the coming of paved roads,
electrification, potable water and sewage systems, altered San Cosme
in the 1960s and 1970s. Those changes, I will suggest, were in many
ways more profound and modernizing than the changes that occurred
there in the 1990s. But it is these later changes, or what is increasingly
referred to as modernity, that seem to capture us—scholars and others in the United States as well as the residents of San Cosme—the
most. Why?

The changes of the 1990s in San Cosme and elsewhere are part of what has come to be called globalization. Regardless of the many different views and definitions of this term, there is widespread agreement that the flows of capital, people, images, commodities, and ideas have intensified tremendously in the last few decades. There is a sense also, both in the popular press and in scholarly discussions, that globalization represents a major transformation in the lives of people everywhere. But the inevitability, desirability, and unevenness of this transformation are contested. Even the most enthusiastic globalists note that there are losers, such as those who are brought into wage labor only to be pushed out when capital moves elsewhere where labor is cheaper. And even critics often seem to accept the inevitability or even the desirability of many of the contemporary changes, although they urge a more equal distribution of the benefits. By following San Cosme over the last half of the twentieth century, the period in which it changed from a peasant to a manufacturing community, we can see how globalization shapes everyday life today and compare it with the shaping effects of what was usually referred to as modernization or development. We can see whether and how globalization is different or is not.

Many scholars and activists have suggested that globalization is a U.S. political project, sometimes called the Washington Consensus. Williamson (2000), the economist who invented that term, notes that it came to mean the series of reforms aimed at increasing the role of market forces by liberalizing trade and financial flows, privatization, and deregulation that U.S. agencies and international financial institutions such as the World Bank and the International Monetary Fund imposed on developing countries. Critics see the Washington Consensus, or what they also refer to as "the globalization project,"[2] as a "neoliberal political ideology that . . . proclaims marketization and privatization as solutions to the world's problems" (Chase-Dunn, Kawano, & Brewer 2000, 77).

But the people of San Cosme are not shaped just by globalization and the projects of outsiders. They have had and continue to have their own political projects. In the past they resisted complete dependence on wages by continuing to practice family agriculture. Today they often resist working for the many global factories near the community. But the world has changed. With increased flows of capital, people, images, commodities, and ideas, the outside is inside San Cosme as never before. Does globalization limit their options and political projects more than development and modernization did? Or can globalization enhance their opportunities for carrying out their own projects?

Modernization, Development, and Globalization: Different Faces of Capitalism

Theories of development, modernization, and globalization have attempted to describe and analyze the kinds of change experienced in San Cosme and communities elsewhere in the developing world over the last fifty years. Globalization theories usually stress connections and flows of people, things, capital, images, and ideas. In this book I assume that important connections have existed among different communities for thousands of years but that the connections that emerged with the rise and spread of capitalism in the late eighteenth century provide the framework for understanding the contemporary world. Until the last two decades, the spread of capitalism was discussed in terms of colonialism, modernization, and development, often without even mentioning capitalism. Whether these theoretical orientations were critical (Frank's [1969] dependency theory, for example, which explained development of the "metropole" as a consequence of the underdevelopment of the "satellite") or were not (Rostow's [1960] theory of stages, which attributed development to internal national characteristics such as consumer production), they projected a pattern of change which was basically linear, with few if any important variations. Some communities were more or less modern than others, but the differences were considered quantitative, not qualitative.[3]

More recently, in what is sometimes called late capitalism (Mandel 1978), disorganized capitalism (Lash and Urry 1987), flexible accumulation (Harvey 1989; Lipietz 1987) or globalization (Appadurai 1996; Kearney 1995; Robertson 1992), profound changes assumed to be different from previous eras are described for the last few decades. These approaches to contemporary capitalism differ as to the nature of the current pattern, whether there is an overall pattern at all, the extent to which the current pattern (or patterns) is (or are) different from other manifestations of capitalism, and what the most significant new aspect(s) of contemporary capitalism might be. All analysts agree, however, that some important changes have occurred so that contemporary capitalist development is indeed different from what capitalism has been. As Jameson pointed out even before globalization became a commonly used term, there is a sense "that something has changed, that things are different, that we have gone through a transformation of the life world which is somehow decisive but incomparable with the older convulsions of modernization and industrialization" (1984, xxi).

The first part of this chapter examines how this transformation has been described and analyzed and suggests that contemporary capitalist processes, like those of the previous two centuries, can best be understood in terms of capitalist accumulation. For Marx, as Wolf (1982, 298) points out, capital accumulation occurs and capitalism emerges when wealth is used to buy labor to produce more wealth. Many analyses of capitalist accumulation, however, have ignored the differences among capitalisms and the unevenness of capitalism.[4] In this book I argue that a more nuanced analysis of capitalist accumulation is necessary. We must incorporate capitalism's unevenness and its power to divide, differentiate, absorb, and expel.[5] Capitalism's unevenness, may mean, for example, that one day workers in Mexico who sell their labor directly to a garment manufacturer quit or lose their jobs and begin to produce similar garments in their own homes. They may then sell garments (and the labor embodied in them, including perhaps the unpaid labor of other family members) directly to that same manufacturer or indirectly through a contractor to a manufacturer or retailer. In each of these scenarios, the workers must sell or give their labor, but the connections (or disconnections) between them and the capitalist are more obvious in the first scenario when they sell their labor directly to the manufacturer. The second scenario of disguised proletarians has the appearance of self-employment, but is one in which individuals have little choice but to sell their product (which is often made to the specifications of the buyer) to the buyer. Unpaid family workers, similarly, must give their labor to their fathers, mothers, spouses or other family members. Thus, workers are differentiated on the basis of a complex relationship between unpaid family workers, disguised proletarians, real proletarians, and capitalists. Later, if the manufacturer, retailer, or contractor goes elsewhere, to China or Swaziland, for example, still another category is generated: expelled workers.[6]

Capital's unevenness has always meant that the relationship between labor and capital, while always based ultimately on the division between those who own the means of production and those who, because they do not have access or sufficient access to the means of production, must sell their labor or depend on others who do so, is more complex than just a simple dichotomy between buyers and sellers of labor power. That capital plays also on existing differences of gender, race, and ethnicity among other factors further complicates the surface picture. The approach I take here recognizes that differentiation among workers exists, but although differences can divide workers, I suggest that differ-

6 Globalization in Rural Mexico

ences may also provide terrains for common struggle. Many analyses give agency to capital and capitalists but not to labor. Often, if labor has agency, it is only in reaction to capitalism. Labor is rarely portrayed as having an agenda and initiatives of its own. Increasingly, it is becoming apparent, however, that there are many people whose agenda is to control, that is, to not sell their labor. Using a variety of techniques, ranging from ignoring or rejecting capitalist alternatives, innovating diverse alternatives (which may derive often from differences that exist among workers as among, for example, part-time workers who also practice family agriculture), as well as occasionally and overtly resisting capitalist alternatives, laborers in San Cosme struggle to shape a better future, if not for themselves then for their children. More and more, their vision of that future does not include wage labor.

In the second part of this chapter, which concerns fieldwork, I suggest that anthropology is well-situated to describe and analyze the complexities of the relationship between capital and labor and the diverse ways that both reveal and use their power. Whereas many approaches, including some that are critical of capitalism, deny workers' agency and see labor as acted upon and as a victim of capitalists' superior arsenal of advantage, anthropology's attention to inside, or emic, views and detailed, local-level accounts can reveal workers' alternative imaginaries and powers to influence outcomes.[7] By looking at the struggle between labor and capital not in the abstract but as exemplified in a real arena and through such an anthropological lens, we can see the subtle as well as more obvious ways in which capitalism and its effects have changed and yet remain the same. And we can see how everyday people cope with and change local and extra-local forces.

Anthropology and Development

The term *globalization* became common in the 1990s, especially in the popular press, international business studies, and international relations. More recently, it has become popular also in anthropology. But the concerns of globalization (about flows of people, products, and so forth), global processes, and interconnections, as Eric Wolf (1982) pointed out more than two decades ago, have been anthropology's concerns since its beginnings. Nineteenth-century evolutionary anthropology, diffusionism, and the neo-evolutionism of Leslie White and Julian Steward were all concerned with the relations between and among people in different communities. Fieldwork, with its emphasis on single communities, and functionalist anthropology, which made a description of the microcosm (the community) an explanation for the macrocosm, shifted attention away from these interconnections (Wolf 1982, 14). Gradually, however, in the postwar period, concern with connections resurfaced in British anthropology with anthropologists of the Manchester School becoming concerned with social change in modern societies and in U.S. anthropology with neo-evolutionism and cultural ecology.[8]

At the same time, in the 1950s and 1960s, the changes associated with postwar independence movements and decolonization and the growth of planned change, or what Escobar (1995) describes as the "discourse and strategy of development," led initially in economics and sociology and later in anthropology to the growth of modernization and development theory. Although development anthropologists usually continued to treat particular communities as isolated in time and space, modernization and development theories implicitly assume connections between the developed and developing (or underdeveloping) worlds. As Frank (1967) pointed out, however, the nature of those connections was never examined. Frank's theory of underdevelopment and dependency theory in general made explicit many of the connections (such as the transfer of wealth from the underdeveloped to the developed) underlying development theory and also argued that those connections, far from being benign or beneficial as assumed in most development theories, were detrimental. As many critics have pointed out, however, dependency theory, with its heavy emphasis on structure, paid little attention to difference and agency.[9] More important, dependency theory does not capture the dynamism of capitalism and the new strategies of capital and labor in capitalism's latest phase at the turn of the new millennium, in what is now called globalization or flexible accumulation.

Focusing on Connections

What distinguishes globalization theory from earlier development theories is that regardless of what variant of it one examines, flows and connections are the focus of attention.[10] In all the discussions of globalization, the emphasis is on movement—of people, commodities, capital, technology, images, and ideas. Many, such as Giddens (1990) and Harvey (1989), try to capture this movement with notions about the compression of time and space. Things and people move faster, more frequently, and farther than ever before. This world in motion has changed and challenged older boundaries of all kinds. Many discussions, for example, especially in sociology and political science where the nation-state has been an important unit of analysis, stress the transnational nature of contemporary flows and the effect of such flows on nation-states. This has led some to talk about the withering and "hollowing out" of the nation-state.[11]

While there seems to be general agreement that today's world is characterized by a compression of time and space, a great deal of disagreement surrounds the extent and significance of the change (or changes) in movement. In part, the disagreement revolves around the baseline and which contemporary conditions are compared. Many who question how new globalization really is and whether movement today is really greater than in the past argue that flows of people or capital only appear greater because past movements are underestimated or ignored. Mintz (1998), for example, argues that people have always been on the move, and Gordon (1988, 63) suggests that we are witnessing a decline in the flow of productive capital. Nevertheless, regardless of such disagreements over how much more people and capital are in motion today, there is agreement that not only do many people move and increasingly imagine moving today but that images and ideas are on the move and with unprecedented velocity.

A major concern of contemporary theorists is not so much whether the flows are greater but which flows are most crucial. Earlier development and modernization theories usually stressed the diffusion of technology and values from the developed to the developing countries and the way internal barriers, such as religious beliefs or personality factors, supposedly prevent modernization. Critical theories, such as dependency theory or Arrighi's (1994) theory of uneven development, focused on the uneven flow of capital and capitalist profits. Like earlier theories of development and modernization, globalization theories vary as to whether causal primacy is given to ideas, material circumstances, production, consumption, class conflict, capital accumulation, and/or any combination of these factors. For Arjun Appadurai (1996), one of the foremost writers on globalization in anthropology and one of the theorists who sees a major transformation, the flow of ideas—through electronic media and migration—and the importance of imagination are what are causal. According to Appadurai, the increased role of imagination, triggered by the movement of images and people, is responsible for what he considers to be qualitative change in the globalized world. For others, such as Daniel Miller (1995b) who concentrates on consumption, the current flow of commodities accounts for the transformation. Still others, such as Basch, Blanc, and Szanton (1994) and those who stress transnationalism, focus on the movement of people who continue to maintain strong ties with their home communities.

Like Harvey and those who follow Marx more closely, this book begins with the struggle between capital and labor and the current form of capital accumulation, what Harvey and others call flexible accumulation. Flexible accumulation refers particularly to the contemporary pattern of the flexible commitment of capital to particular places and workers. It involves a more frequent movement of productive capital and threat of movement to new places and new workers as well as more frequent movement of finance capital to new markets. Consequently, for me, the flow of capital is crucial but not all-powerful. Even if capitalist production can shift from place to place at any given time, it must take place somewhere. At those particular times and in those places, what really happens is an outcome of the struggle between capital and labor. Thus, capital's paths and the strategies of capitalists are consequences of the struggle between capital and labor at particular times in particular places.

When I look at contemporary flows of capital, people, commodities, images and ideas, what strikes me most is the diversity and unevenness one sees in the contemporary world. Huge amounts of capital flow today to China, for example. But to Zambia or elsewhere in Africa the flow of capital has almost stopped.[12] Today, also, the direction of capital flow varies widely. Capital flows not only within the North and from the North to the South but also from the South to the North and within the South. Capitalist investment in particular places also varies. Capital flows into Fordist production, post-Fordist production, and no production (that is, into services and financial markets).

Most discussions of capital flow assume its enormous power to go wherever, whenever, and for whatever purposes capitalists want. Capitalists' success with trade liberalization in the last two decades has certainly advanced their interests and reinforced a view of capital's limitless power. That capitalists needed to pursue a new tactic, however, was due in part to labor's successful struggle to improve working conditions and living standards during the postwar period in many parts of both the North and South. In the developed world, labor successfully pressed for higher wages, security, and expanded state benefits—all of which affected capital's profits. In developing countries, such as Mexico and many others, import-substitution industrialization (often tied to populist state policies) restricted imports to encourage national industrial development, thus limiting the flow of commodities from the advanced capitalist countries. Many developing countries, including Mexico, also placed some limits on foreign investment. Consequently, although commodities and capital often got through protectionist barriers, capitalists did not have complete freedom of choice in where and how to invest or market.

Capital, as Harvey (1989) points out, has always had its "spatial fixes." Crises of overaccumulation or surplus capital have often been addressed through geographical expansion. That capital has had to look for spatial fixes and where it finds its fixes depends on labor and the relation between the two. As Cowie stresses in his important study of the RCA Corporation's movements and site selection process throughout the twentieth century, "the evolving social history of working people was at the center of the story" (1999, 6).

The search for greater profitability by capitalists as it conflicts with the desire for better living conditions for working people includes the movement of people as well as capital. Here, too, I am struck by the diversity in patterns of movement and the often neglected but critical role of labor in determining its own movements. Discussions of migration often focus on labor's movements in relation to capital's whereabouts and, more recently, in reaction to capital's threats to move. Perhaps because I see so much through the lens of what San Cosmeros/as do, in the new millennium I see not only more movement but also greater movement being replaced by less movement. Today, while many people are on the move, many are not. Additionally, many who were on the move now stay put. Men from San Cosme migrated in large numbers weekly to Mexico City during the 1960s and 1970s. But very few moved permanently to the Federal District. Today those same men and their sons rarely migrate temporarily, seasonally, weekly, or permanently for work. Instead, they remain in the community and work, often right in their own homes. That they can remain in the community is due largely to the pattern of return or weekly migration they maintained earlier that allowed their ties and lives in the community to persist. Because they returned regularly to their families and their family agriculture, they retained kinship ties and alternative subsistence strategies that in the 1990s and today provide a base on which to build their garment production and other commercial and professional alternatives.

Today also, some women who, to borrow a phrase from Carolyn Brettell (1986), waited at home while men migrated now move—daily, weekly, or permanently—for work or study. But women also resist moving. As indicated in Chapter 5, although many women are now employed, few from San Cosme choose to work outside the community. Elsewhere, numerous differences, unevenness, and variations also characterize people's movements. Although the immigrant population of the United States has increased (Kilborn & Clemetson 2002), immigrants now come from different places and go to different places within the United States, and many immigrate elsewhere; for example, they move from Asia to the Middle East.

Where capital is invested plays a major role in forcing people from subsistence economies into wage labor and, thus, in pushing labor to migrate. But capital flow is a changing process that, as indicated above, does not always and inevitably unfold in the same way in every place. One of the themes of this book is that the continued maintenance of kinship and subsistence practices by San Cosmeros/as has enabled and encouraged them to sometimes resist wage labor, sometimes ignore capitalist wage relations, and sometimes to reconfigure wage relations. For them, moving has thus been not simply a matter of where the jobs are but also what other options they have created or can create for themselves. The flow of capital influences their movements, but so too do social relations that derive from a different noncapitalist, subsistence imaginary. That noncapitalist imaginary sees family reproduction as more important than capitalist profit. I am not proposing a culture among San Cosmeros/as that produces a different capitalism or a noncapitalist pattern. As Yanigasako argues, "Culture does not produce capitalism; *people* produce capitalism. . . ." (2002, 188; emphasis added). People also produce noncapitalism. To do so, however, they need lived experiences or recent memories of alternative practices on which to build alternative visions. Among factory workers in China, for example, memories of spatial relations are not erased by newer epistemes stressing efficiency (Rofel 1993, 96). Workers "questioned and contested the new authority of efficiency with memories of previous spatial relations . . . Through these memories, they created spaces of subversion, both subtle and direct" (Rofel 1993, 99). Because until recently almost all San Cosmeros/as lived a life based on the family economy, the basis for a noncapitalist vision persists.

As I have indicated, some theories of globalization stress the flow of ideas, images, or commodities. Here, too, I am struck by variation and unevenness. While millions of people throughout the world see the same images and wear the same jeans, millions do not. Some people have access to computers, televisions, VCRs, and print media, but many others do not. Capital (through its control of the media, advertising, and markets) structures much of the flow of ideas, images, and commodities and, like other flows it affects, it does so unevenly. Additionally, as with the movement of capital and people, goods, images, and ideas are resisted, ignored, and reconfigured.

Focusing on the flow of capital while keeping in mind that it cannot go wherever or whenever it wants incorporates the notion that there are diverse and unequal flows of capital, people, commodities, images, and ideas. In this book I follow Harvey and stress the flow of capital, especially changes in the accumulation of finance capital and the liberalization of financial flows and the flexibilization of labor, as the central factors in globalization. It is important to note, however, that finance capital is not (despite the efforts of neoliberal strategists, millennial capitalists, or global financial conjurers) the only or the common pattern in all contexts even today.[13] Flexibilization (which itself consists of a variety of practices) is similarly not found to the same extent everywhere. Furthermore, it is not, as is frequently assumed, found only in post-Fordist production (Collins 2000). How labor responds—and how capital envisions labor's response—in particular places also varies in crucial ways.

Anthropology has the potential to deepen our understanding of these complexities and differences. Anthropology's attention to detail and insider views provides an important basis on which to look at global flows without assuming or projecting a single hegemonic pattern. But anthropology must also look at broader patterns. How we can look at both the specific and the general is the subject of the next section.

Anthropology, Ethnographic Fieldwork, and Globalization

As indicated above, the concerns of globalization—global processes and interconnections—have always been anthropology's concerns. For much of the twentieth century, however, the practice of fieldwork seemed to encourage anthropologists to focus on a particular community and, except for some of the earlier Boasians who were concerned with diffusion, to treat that community as if it were isolated in time and space. Because fieldwork stressed immersion in the community, few theorized about those relations, even when in the second half of the twentieth century many anthropologists became aware of the importance of looking at extralocal relations, as Roseberry (1989) points out. Rather than using a deductive approach beginning with theory, anthropologists placed themselves in a particular community and followed their informants out of the community (Rothstein 1982). At times we tried to locate the specific places we studied in the world by using dependency or other macrotheories, but the focus of anthropological research, even in these broader studies, remained a particular community and how extralocal relations influenced that community. What happened in the communities we studied was rarely seen as affecting extralocal relations, or if we did note such effects those effects were not theorized.

In the 1970s and 1980s, a growing number of anthropologists began using class to link local and extralocal processes.[14] But the possibilities of class analysis were not pursued in mainstream anthropology, and much of it remained rooted in the study of presumably isolated and homogeneous communities for which the potential of class analysis remained unrecognized.

Today, in response to the awareness of questions raised by our own research that went unanswered by the data gathered in single communities and to an increasing perception that the world has changed—in part because of the popular discussion of globalization and in part owing to the increasing presence of the people we have studied in the places we live and work—there is a growing body of anthropological literature from which intensive study of a single community has disappeared. In some contemporary analyses, fieldwork seems to have almost completely vanished.[15] Other analyses use what Marcus (1998, 81) calls "multi-sited" ethnography in which "strategies of quite literally following connections, associations, and putative relationships are . . . at the very heart of designing multi-sited ethnographic research" in diverse places linked by the global flows of people, ideas, commodities, capital, and images. Multi-sited ethnography retains fieldwork, but—like the inductive approach of Oscar Lewis and others who in the 1950s and 1960s followed migrants to towns, cities, and beyond—it puts fieldwork before theory.[16]

By not beginning with a theory of the world or the larger whole, as the sociologist Michael Burawoy has suggested, anthropologists "open up their studies to the world, without the world's becoming an object of investigation" (Burawoy 2000, 29). We should continue to do field-work and to follow connections that emerge in the field, but fieldwork will be more productive if we understand what connections are likely to emerge and why. That is, we need to begin with a notion of what the connections might be. It is here that the recent theories and conceptualizations of globalization may be useful. They can help us to address the questions posed in the beginning of this chapter. What is globalization? Is it new or different? Is it inevitable? Who benefits from globalization and who does not? In this approach, theory is used to guide ethnography and fieldwork. Then the revelations that come from immersion into particular ways of life and listening to diverse views of life can refine, refute, and verify theoretical conceptions at higher levels of generalization.

It is important to stress that a community-based approach, guided by theory, does not confine itself to research in the community. For theoretical and empirical reasons, the field-worker does leave a particular community. My fieldwork was centered in San Cosme, but I went with San Cosmeros/as to many sites in the states of Tlaxcala and Puebla and in the Federal District. At times my travel with them brought me also to various places in other Mexican states and New York City. For theoretical reasons, I (or an assistant) also went to the state capital of Tlaxcala to interview people on state economic development, union organization, and foreign investment and to Mexico City to interview national and regional politicians on state policy and power. I also spoke with garment manufacturers in the United States about their outsourcing strategies. While I do not think a community study approach alone is adequate, it is important to note that multi-sited ethnography is often stretched too thin to provide the detail and nuanced insider views which are a great part of anthropology's strength. Furthermore, multi-sited research may illuminate only certain strands of global connectivity and overlook that which is not so connected.

Fieldwork over Time

This book is based on very intensive immersion into a single community in rural Mexico, San Cosme Mazatecochco. But it is also guided by broader theoretical concerns. For me personally and intellectually, San Cosme and the people there have been a major part of my life and the life of my family for more than thirty years. In all I have spent more than two and a half years living in the community during eight field visits. Over the years, understanding San Cosme has also required a "multi-sited research imaginary" (Marcus 1998, 3), that is, leaving the community—physically and emotionally. Sometimes it required visiting people from San Cosme at their factories in Mexico City or Puebla, visiting their politicians in Tlaxcala or Mexico City, and, more recently, visiting with San Cosmeros/as living in New York City and New Jersey. Sometimes it meant migrating weekly, as many of the residents in San Cosme do, to Mexico City. It has also meant reading the *New York Times* (especially the business sections), the *Wall Street Journal, La Jornada, El Financero, Sol de Tlaxcala,* and Mexican government documents—all and always with San Cosme in mind.

But wherever people from San Cosme are and wherever they are directly or indirectly discussed, understanding what they are doing and why required a broad view, a theoretical conceptualization of the local, national, and global processes and struggles that pushed and pulled people in various directions. Whether they involved peasants producing for subsistence in their own community, homemakers taking care of their houses and families, children studying in a nearby city, factory workers in textile factories in Mexico City, merchants selling garments in regional markets, or a San Cosmera coming to New York to buy South African ostrich feathers for Carnival headdresses, the processes and struggles of capitalist accumulation were at work and, if one looked, discernible. These processes and struggles neither began nor ended in San Cosme or even in Mexico. But they always took me back to San Cosme where I could see how they played out. Thus, while I sometimes separate theory and method for discussion purposes, I see the processes and struggles of capitalist accumulation enacted by people. Ethnographic fieldwork is a way to see, hear, and experience those enactments. Although anthropologists, like everyone else, experience those processes every day everywhere—at work, at home, and at play— fieldwork, especially long-term fieldwork, heightens and deepens one's awareness of those processes.

I am not suggesting that ethnographic research in one's own community on other kinds of research is not useful. Harvey (2000), for example, has been particularly sensitive to the everyday enactments of capital accumulation in his descriptions and analyses of Baltimore. Likewise, native anthropologists have often been more insightful to local interpretations and views than outsiders have been. However, native anthropologists may overlook what they are accustomed to, and people may not tell them about some practices or beliefs, assuming they are familiar with the culture (Jones 1970).

This book is based on such long-term fieldwork in a community in a setting different from where I live. I first went to San Cosme from Pittsburgh as a graduate student in 1971 because I was interested in political factionalism (not capital accumulation, which was rarely discussed in the anthropological literature of my graduate school days). San Cosme is in a region characterized by the kind of change that seemed to surround factions wherever they had been reported.[17] Leaders with whom I spoke when I arrived in Tlaxcala, the state capital, described San Cosme as a divisive community, a description that suggested the kind of factionalism in which I was interested. Although I did study factionalism, the changes that had contributed to the political divisiveness came to appear even more important than the factionalism itself. These changes were tied to increased dependence on wage work, as men from families with too little land went off to work in the national textile industry in Mexico City or Puebla. Factory work enabled a handful of men, usually union leaders, to get some political power in the local arena. Since none of the leaders had enough power to control more than a fraction of the workers and since the Mexican political structure limited the kinds of gains that could be sought and offered, leaders recruited their followers along diverse lines, including coworkers in the same factory as well as kinship and neighborhood ties, rather than according to issues or party lines.

Although factory work was related to factionalism and divisions within the community, it also led to community improvements. Through their factory work and with the help of their families, neighbors, and regional political leaders, men from San Cosme brought roads, buses, electricity, potable water, schools, and health and other services to the community, as well as factionalism.

Perhaps the most important consequence of factory work was the hope that emerged in the 1960s and early 1970s that the future for children would be better than the past had been for their parents. Parents especially hoped that through more education their children would experience mobility. Even then, however, during what has come to be referred to as the Mexican economic miracle and when some standard indicators of economic progress grew at a dizzying rate (Anderson 1968, 178–179), some San Cosmeros/as (and critics of the Mexican development pattern) saw limits in capitalist growth. Although sons and daughters of peasants who had became proletarians usually experienced some gains, many of the second generation of proletarians saw a future for themselves as proletarians like their parents, with little hope for anything better. Signs of such discontent were evident in the formation of several new local branches of left political parties, including the Mexican Communist Party (PCM) and the Mexican Workers Party (PMT).

When I was trying to describe and understand the weekly and daily movement of wage workers to Mexico City or Puebla for factory jobs, my analysis relied heavily on dependency theory. I argued that change in San Cosme needed to be viewed in terms of the larger capitalist system and especially Mexico's dependent capitalism. I saw the greater poverty and concentration of wealth that characterized dependent capitalism—because much of the profits were transferred elsewhere—as even more limiting of upward mobility than advanced capitalism (Rothstein 1982, 129). Although I saw much of what was happening in San Cosme in terms of capitalism and described San Cosmeros/as as proletarians, I had not yet made the connection between proletarians in San Cosme and those elsewhere in Mexico and other parts of the world.

In the early 1980s I returned to San Cosme to study the discontent with the Mexican development model that had surfaced in the community in the late 1970s. In addition to the appearance of left political parties toward the end of the 1970s, San Cosmeros/as had resisted the state's efforts to buy their lands for the construction of private firms. When I arrived in 1984, however, I found that although many of the new parties were still there (the PRI, the dominant party in Mexico until recently, has never gone uncontested in San Cosme since), what was of greatest concern to the residents of San Cosme was the economic crisis that had come to a head in Mexico in 1982. Everybody in San Cosme talked about *el crisis*. They talked about lost jobs as factories closed, declining wages for those who kept their jobs, and the rising cost of living. They were not talking much about politics or mobility. They were talking about how to make ends meet. Consequently, as anthropologists do (and as I had done earlier when I broadened my interest in factionalism to proletarianization), I shifted my research agenda to what concerned San Cosmeros/as—feeding, clothing, and sheltering their families daily.

At the same time that San Cosmeros/as were focusing on how to survive the economic crisis, theoretical discussion by critical economists, sociologists, and anthropologists was increasingly linking capitalism in the North and the South with sharper new (or revived older) concepts and analyses. Studies of the growth of manufacturing for export, the new international division of labor, and structural adjustment policies made clearer than ever the nature of the connections around the world.[18] These studies pointed to the growth of offshore production as multinational corporations from the United States, Japan, and Western Europe relocated to developing countries, including Mexico, where wages were lower and regulations, such as environmental protections or health and safety rules, were less stringent or less well-enforced. This new international division of labor, encouraged especially by the structural adjustment policies of the World Bank and the International Monetary Fund, allowed multinational corporations to reap greater profits. While many of these studies saw what happened in the developing world largely as a result of the requirements of capital accumulation, some began to give more attention to local forces, structures, and agency. Increasingly, anthropologists especially have looked at class and diverse forms of struggle and resistance, ranging from spirit possession (Ong 1987) and environmental organization (Susser 1992) to labor uprisings (Kim 1992).

While some San Cosmeros/as did participate in strikes and other overt forms of collective protest, during the 1980s San Cosmeros/as dealt with the crisis primarily through household patterns of multiple livelihoods, including increased reliance on the products they themselves could produce, such as corn. They also practiced huddling (living in larger households), and more household members got involved in income generation (Rothstein 1995). During a brief visit to San Cosme in the summer of 1993, I heard about a new income-generating activity. A number of people had bought sewing machines and were making garments. I saw a garment workshop for the first time during that two-day visit while on my way to a conference. By the mid-1990s, when I returned, hundreds of families in San Cosme had settled on a new way to make a living: small-scale garment manufacturing. Since then, that industry has taken over the community, and in the last ten years I, too, have begun to focus on garment production. Understanding the extent and significance of the change was made easier for me because over many years I had observed San Cosmeros/as in kinship, religious, political, and economic activities and listened to them talk about their hopes, plans, expectations, and worries. The new theoretical approaches that linked people throughout the world in a new global system without seeing them as mere pawns in a capitalist game has facilitated seeing the complexities of San Cosmeros/as responses. Although they must act within a global capitalist world, that is not the only world they know about or the only one that provides visions of the future.

This book tells the story of my involvement in San Cosme's enactments and visions during the last three decades. Our connections, especially when I am not there, have changed, thus paralleling the changes that have taken place elsewhere and which are the subject of much of the globalization discussion. My involvement with San Cosmeros/as now is more constant. I speak to people from San Cosme by telephone regularly and I know that I can pick up the phone and call San Cosme at any time. I occasionally see someone from San Cosme in New York and I communicate with a San Cosme woman via the Internet. Most of all I am always aware of the interconnectedness of our lives and the extent to which people in San Cosme and people in the United States and elsewhere are connected. Whether it is the Mexicans I see often on the streets of New York, the products made in Mexico that I see constantly, or articles in a New York newspaper on Wal-Mart's share of the Mexican market or on the opening of a Tiffany store in Puebla, I am constantly reminded of these interconnections.

In the past when I went to San Cosme, like its residents I was relatively isolated from the larger world. In the early 1970s we rarely got mail from the United States and to do so we needed to go to a post office about half an hour away. To speak to anyone in the United States we needed to go to Puebla. Getting a long-distance phone call through was always a difficult and often an unsuccessful process. During my recent stay in 2001, I spoke to family in New York all the time from the house where I was living or from a phone on the main plaza. I heard about the attack on the World Trade Center within minutes from someone who heard about it on his radio, and we saw television coverage at the same time as viewers in New York. During the weeks and months that followed, images and discussions of the attack and then the U.S. war on Afghanistan were constant and everywhere in San Cosme. Everyone I met in San Cosme or elsewhere in Mexico who recognized me as from the United States and who knew about the attack and the war always raised the subject. They always offered their sympathy for what they all saw as a terrible tragedy. Sometimes also they criticized the U.S. war in Afghanistan; sometimes they expressed concern for the safety of my family and friends. As time went on, people began expressing fears about their own security and the economic effects of 9/11 on Mexico and Mexicans.

In the chapters that follow, I try to convey a sense of the connections between San Cosmeros/as and others, their awareness of these connections, and how both the connections and their awareness of them have changed over the last few decades. As the connections of San Cosmeros/as to each other and with people elsewhere (including me) have changed, theories about connections have also changed. Geopolitical changes and the neglect by many older approaches of the ways in which people such as those in San Cosme innovate and influence the world around them have led me to find the theoretical formulation that Harvey bases on Marx to be most useful. I build on Harvey's suggestion (2000, 79) that we need to think across scales and not lock ourselves into a single one, whether it be local or global. Thus, while I focus on the residents of San Cosme, I look also at other, larger processes.

In the next chapter I describe some of the broad patterns of connections involving San Cosme, Mexico, U.S. capitalism, and the world during the last half of the twentieth century. Chapter 3 examines how these broader patterns interact with local configurations. It begins with a discussion of the family economy in the early 1970s and goes on to describe how development contributed to a process of de-peasantization (but not to the disappearance of the family economy) and to the emergence of a community of industrial factory workers and their families. The chapter ends with the decline of factory work and the appearance of small-scale garment production. Chapter 4 describes that garment industry. In Chapter 5 I look at the intersection of kinship, gender, age, and flexible production and how workers and owners are responding to a system of production that has no commitment to places, things, or people. Chapter 6 examines consumerism, one of these responses. Many recent studies have seen in contemporary workers' consumerist practices a new global pattern that shifts the engine of the global economy from production to consumption. I question this view. Consumers, as a recent *New York Times* article on NAFTA pointed out, are also workers (Weiner 2003). I argue that the new consumerism hides the importance of production relations and that capitalist relations of production are, if anything, more important today than ever.

In the concluding chapter I return to broader notions of connections and closeness. I argue that globalization is not really very different from development or colonialism, two earlier forms of capitalist domination. But I argue also that the same modern technology—electronic communication and cheaper transportation—that capitalists use to reap their profits in more flexible ways can and is being used also by labor,

Figure 1.1. Calle Principal (Main Street), 1971

Figure 1.2. Calle Principal Monday garment market, 2004

sometimes in reaction to capital but also to pursue alternative agendas that derive from other imaginaries. To appreciate the new potential of labor and alternative visions of what the future might be like, we need to broaden our concept of labor and recognize the multiple sites where it can struggle. We need also to focus—in theory and practice—on what connects workers within workplaces, in different workplaces, and in different work situations to each other.

CHAPTER 2

Mexico and the World

In a recent discussion of anthropological community studies, June Nash comments that when she first went to Amatenango, a rural community in Chiapas in the late 1950s, it was easy to see why anthropologists accepted the residents' view that the community was the center of the universe (2001, 33). In her analysis of Amatenango, she found it was not possible to see the community without considering its larger context, but within it there were "no telephones, buses, or newspapers to distract people with an imagined nation or world beyond that" (2001, 33).

When I first went to San Cosme in the early 1970s, my experience was very similar. Life there, although clearly structured by the larger Mexican political economy, was also viewed by residents as centered in their community. While I was theoretically prepared to recognize the importance of what Eric Wolf (1956) called "extra-community relations," like Nash I felt a sense of boundedness within the community. This was reinforced by a circular pattern of weekly migration by many of the men of the community to their factory jobs in Mexico City. Each week, hundreds went there to work in textile factories, but on the weekends they returned to San Cosme. Most of the men married women from San Cosme (even if they had another wife or girlfriend in Mexico City), participated in local politics, and bought land and tended fields in San Cosme. The factories with the largest number of workers from the community provided buses that went directly from the community to the factory and back every week. In Mexico City the men usually worked with others from San Cosme. Most had gotten their jobs through kin, neighbors, and friends from San Cosme, and most shared housing with others from the community. Very few moved permanently to Mexico City or even conceived of wanting to move there permanently.

But they did go to Mexico City or Puebla for factory work, though their parents had not. To understand why they went and how their trips beyond the community affected them, their kin, and neighbors, it is necessary to look beyond the local community to Mexican political economy and its relation to the world.

A Brief History

Most of the residents of San Cosme are descendants of the Tlaxcalans who were living in the region when the Spanish arrived in the sixteenth century. After their own defeat by the Spanish, the Tlaxcalans helped Cortes defeat the Aztecs. In return for their aid and through an active struggle to secure privilege, the Tlaxcalans fared somewhat better than other indigenous groups in postconquest Mexico.[1] By the beginning of the twentieth century, however, land in Tlaxcala had become increasingly concentrated in the hands of a small number of mostly *criollo* or *mestizo hacienda* owners while a larger, indigenous majority owned little or no land. In San Cosme most of the land was concentrated into four *haciendas* on which the indigenous population worked as peons.

As a result of the Mexican Revolution (1910–1917), many Tlaxcalans received *ejidos* (land granted under the agrarian reform). In San Cosme, the residents had purchased small parcels of land from the local *hacendados* before the government began granting *ejidos*. Thus, the residents of San Cosme own their small parcels of land rather than being *ejidatarios*. For several decades these small landowners were able to subsist on their plots, cultivating squash, beans, and corn and working as seasonal workers for neighbors in the nearby town of San Francisco Papalotla.

Even by 1950, according to the national census, 90 percent of the population walked barefoot and 85 percent spoke Nahuatl. Except for a few families that supplemented agriculture with a mill or general store and a handful of factory workers, the people of San Cosme were *campesinos* who relied primarily on subsistence agriculture. This relatively homogeneous community was to change greatly, however, as the Mexican state increasingly pursued a policy of capitalist development.

Despite the Mexican Revolution and its populist rhetoric of development and support for the masses, the Mexican state, especially since the 1940s, has followed a path of capitalist development that has increasingly favored the few (including foreigners) over the majority. State programs supported industrial growth over agriculture and favored large-scale commercial agriculture over small-scale subsistence cultivation. Consequently, small-scale cultivators, or peasants like those in San Cosme, received little support from the government, and state policies often hurt them.

State Policies and the Global Economy: 1940s–1970s

Recent Mexican history is usefully viewed in terms of three periods: Cárdenas's "nationalist-populist" period in the 1930s (Cypher 1990, 10); import substitution industrialization from the 1940s to the 1970s; and, since the 1980s, neoliberalism. Each of these periods represents increased integration into the global economy.

President Cárdenas laid the foundation for subsequent capitalist development, but his more nationalist and populist approach kept the world at a greater distance. He favored a national over the international bourgeoisie, a mixed approach relying on public and private capital accumulation to finance industrial development, and he encouraged an organized peasantry and working class to have political input at the national level through influential sectors of the Institutional Revolutionary Party (PRI), the ruling party. The Depression, which reduced international trade, Cárdenas's support of labor, and his expropriation of the foreign-owned oil industry, left Mexico less dependent on other countries, especially the United States, than at almost any other time since the fifteenth century. Direct foreign investment, for example, dropped from 3.5 billion pesos in 1926 to 2.6 billion pesos in 1939 (Hansen 1971, 30). The basic capitalist development pattern of a society divided between capitalists and labor, however, while modified to some extent, remained in effect.

During the Second World War, fueled by U.S. war needs, Mexican agribusiness, industry, and mining grew significantly (Barkin 1986, 115; Cypher 1990, 45). This growth put Mexico back into a more dependent relationship with the United States and, with support from Mexican state policies, helped to consolidate a new national Mexican elite:

A [new] revolutionary elite grew in close association with government policies. War contracts, tax breaks, falling real wages, a regressive tax structure and monetary favors all constituted the increased role of the

State in the process of capital accumulation. (Niblo 1988, 34; cited by Cypher 1990, 49)

During the 1940s, 1950s, and 1960s, capital investment (including foreign capital investment), especially in commercial agriculture and industry, grew significantly. The Mexican state played a central role in this development. It maintained a politically stable environment suitable for capital investment and used public sector financing to encourage capitalist development and provide infrastructural support for that development. To protect its capitalist class as well as its national industry, Mexico—like many other developing countries at the time and like developed countries in earlier stages of their industrialization that were faced with the competition of older, more advanced industrialized countries—adopted a policy of import substitution industrialization (ISI). The aim of ISI "was to protect a nation's infant industries so that the overall industrial structure could be developed and diversified and dependence on foreign technology and capital reduced" (Dicken 1998, 127). ISI protects a country's industrial growth by placing tariffs on imported goods as well as supporting national industrialization with various incentives. This supposedly "inward-oriented industrialized policy," to borrow the term used by Dicken (142), actually led Mexico to increased imports of the machinery, for example, that would be used in manufacturing and therefore to dependence, especially technological dependence, principally on the United States. Although Mexican industrial output did grow, imports grew more. Whereas output increased five times between 1940 and 1965, imports of industrial or capital goods and replacement parts, mainly from the United States, increased 12.5 times (Cockcroft 1990, 161–162). Initially, the capital invested to promote industrialization was largely public savings from the public sector, domestic savings, and domestic borrowing (Hansen 1971, 46).[2] Beginning in the 1950s, Mexico began to rely more on foreign investment (Cockcroft 1990, 161) and foreign borrowing (Hansen 1971, 46).[3] Between 1960 and 1968, the total book value of private foreign investment increased by more than 100 percent, from $1.08 billion to $2.3 billion (Wionczek 1974 cited by Barkin 1986, 116). During that period also, foreign indebtedness grew considerably. Between 1960 and 1969, public foreign debt with a maturity of greater than one year increased from $842 million to $3.511 billion (Barkin 1986, 121). By the end of the 1970s, therefore, Mexico was much more integrated into the global economy through foreign investment, trade, and foreign borrowing than it had been during the Cárdenas nationalist-populist period. Despite what was often referred to as "miraculous economic growth," the trade deficit, the income that foreign investors withdrew from Mexico, and payments on foreign borrowing meant that a huge part of the domestically produced surplus was transferred out of Mexico, mostly to the United States (Rothstein 1979, 27).[4] Capitalism, by its nature, distributes rewards unequally. Dependent capitalism, in which much of the domestically produced surplus goes elsewhere, produces even more inequality between developing and developed countries, thus defying the promises of modernization theory that the spread of industrial technology would narrow that gap.

The transfer of a large part of the domestically produced surplus (to repay foreign debts and as profit to foreign investors) had enormous consequences for the Mexican class structure and for the distribution of the benefits of Mexican industrialization and the so-called Mexican economic miracle. It is generally conceded that the poor were relatively better off in 1940 before the miracle than in 1970 (Barkin 1986, 107).[5] In 1969, the income share of the poorest 50 percent of Mexican families was only 15 percent compared with 19 percent in 1950 (Barkin 1986, Table 4.1). However, although they did not benefit nearly as much as the rich, some of the poor and the middle class did benefit absolutely, if not relatively. Like other rural Mexicans, many of the residents of San Cosme did not benefit from the economic miracle; others, however, were able to take advantage of some of the possibilities that emerged during the boom following World War II.

The "Miracle" in San Cosme

As a result of the Mexican government's support of industrialization, some infrastructure development occurred in Tlaxcala and industry grew, especially in the Federal District only sixty miles away.[6] Men of San Cosme were able to find industrial jobs in the expanding national textile industry. But that they turned to industry from agriculture was at least in part because of the lack of dynamic in peasant agriculture and the state's neglect of small-scale agriculture. Most of the men, therefore, who became *obreros* (factory workers) were pushed out of agriculture and into full-time industrial wage work.

Beginning in 1940, the Mexican state consistently favored new industrial and commercial agricultural elites over the peasant sector. Between

1940 and 1970, direct public investment went disproportionately to the industrial sector (Hansen 1971, 45). Public policies, including protective tariffs, licensing agreements, credit, import privileges, tax concessions, and a fiscal policy favoring price increases and inflation rather than taxes, supported the industrial sector. The advantages given to capitalist industry led to huge increases in productivity and large profits. Average growth rates in manufacturing production were consistently high throughout the 1940s, 1950s, and 1960s (Hansen 1971, 42).

Agricultural productivity also increased during the Mexican miracle but primarily in larger, private landholdings (Hansen 1971, 61). Despite the fact that the vast majority of Mexico's landholdings were smallholdings, the state's policy favored larger holdings. Massive irrigation projects, exemptions from further expropriation of irrigated land or land in specified crops such as export crops like cotton and coffee, and credit and technological improvement programs all favored capitalist agriculture over the peasant or *minifundista* sector (Hansen 1971, 58–65).

In the early 1970s, San Cosme was an excellent example of the strains in Mexico's smallholding sector. Families in San Cosme averaged less than five hectares of land. The few who had more, about five families with fifteen hectares each, would shortly subdivide their larger holdings among their children. Few families had access to irrigation and almost all practiced plow culture focusing on subsistence production with corn as the principal and sometimes only crop. Access to credit was limited to moneylenders charging high rates of interest. The possibilities of changing their methods of cultivation and/or crops and increasing productivity were extremely limited. The few who had tried to increase their productivity encountered enormous difficulties. Those who had access to a little more cash might try to invest in animals such as cows, pigs, or chickens or in new technology such as chemical fertilizer or new seeds. Often, however, their animals died or the returns from the added investment proved inconsistent at best. In 1971, Don Pedro and Doña Margarita invested in two pigs only to find their piglets dead at birth. Another woman traveled by bus for an hour to where the government was selling chickens at reduced prices. Most of her chickens died of suffocation on the trip back to San Cosme.

Given the lack of dynamic in small-scale agriculture, each year more and more families needed to supplement their subsistence production with more wage labor. Men from neighboring communities, such as San Francisco Papalotla, the municipality of which San Cosme was originally a part, had worked in the textile industry in Tlaxcala for many years. In part because they had enough land for subsistence and in part because the people of Papalotla kept them out of the local factories, men from San Cosme had rarely worked in Tlaxcalan factories.

As a result of the national textile boom during the Second World War and the stagnation in small-scale agriculture, during the 1940s some men from San Cosme began working in textile factories in Mexico City, about sixty miles away, or in Puebla, ten miles away. Initially, only a few men went to work in factories, but as the value of their agricultural production declined and land pressure mounted, the number of factory workers, especially textile workers, grew to almost half of the economically active men in 1980 (Rothstein 1995, Table 7-5).

As will be discussed in Chapter 3, many of San Cosme's factory workers were able to use their wages, supplemented by subsistence cultivation, to invest in taxis, trucks, stores, land, and their children's education. Through the contacts they made in the factories, they were able to change San Cosme's political status from a section of the municipality of San Francisco Papalotla to a free municipality. They struggled for and successfully obtained services such as potable water, electricity, more schools, bus service, and improved roads.

The state's support of industrialization, specifically import substitution at this time, thus provided some opportunities for some of the people of San Cosme. But the benefits were very unevenly distributed. Households without factory workers—those that relied on agriculture and sporadic, usually informal sector wagework—fared poorly. Women, who were excluded from the factory jobs that the men got, became dependent on men for cash. Factory work increased the gap between women and men and between *campesinos* and workers. The nature of relations between San Cosme and the world beyond its borders also changed. Although the lives of most San Cosmeros/as continued to revolve around the community, their jobs, political decisions, and schooling and other opportunities were all increasingly interwoven with regional and national policies, including national policies affecting international relations. Residents of San Cosme benefited differentially from this changed integration, but all were affected by the community's greater integration into the Mexican nation and the nation's greater integration into the world.

Import substitution industrialization (and the increased economic integration it involved) eventually ended in what was known in Mexico as *el crisis*, which brought on new forms of global integration. During the 1980s, in what has come to be referred to as the lost decade, even the minimal absolute benefits accruing to the poor and many of the advantages gained by the middle class were lost. For the people of San Cosme, textile factory jobs and the professional jobs as teachers, nurses, and doctors that their children were beginning to get disappeared. Some women and men trained as teachers waited years for teaching positions or accepted placement very far away. Men who managed to keep their factory jobs saw their wages and work conditions deteriorate. Many had their hours reduced. As the crisis became today's neoliberalism or globalization, the residents of San Cosme sought new ways to survive and, when possible, to prosper. More than ever, their solutions are woven from a web of connections that go way beyond the community. Although sometimes this new integration leaves San Cosmeros/as in a more vulnerable position, these connections may also offer the potential for greater control.

Neoliberalism: The Crisis and Its Solution

There is a great deal of disagreement over the main causes of the economic crisis that erupted in 1982 when Mexico announced that it could not pay its debts to international creditors. Much of the blame has been put on import substitution industrialization. Critics, many of whom had supported ISI and who often ignore protectionism in the developed countries, argue that protected industries lack incentives to become more efficient and productive. Those who had criticized Mexico's miracle from the beginning point not to ISI but to the draining of so much of the country's economic surplus to fuel capital accumulation elsewhere, especially in the United States, and the pronounced inequality and growing class conflict that developed from that pattern of accumulation.[7] Most analysts also stress more immediate causes, including Mexico's dependence on the export of oil and the drop in oil prices in the early 1980s, along with rising interest rates and capital flight.

Whatever one's view of the causes of Mexico's crisis, it did prompt a profound economic restructuring and transformation. Mexico's threatened debt default in 1982 precipitated a call by the United States, the International Monetary Fund (IMF), and the World Bank for a series of structural adjustment policies (SAPs) that included austerity, privatization, trade liberalization, and export-oriented industrial production. Whereas ISI had protected and promoted national industries and national consumption, manufacturing for export opened Mexico up to increased foreign investment in industrial production for the international market. Eventually, many other countries experienced a similar debt crisis, and the United States, the IMF and the World Bank also pressured them to adopt similar structural adjustment or neoliberal policies. When interest rates rose and the prices of exports such as oil declined, many developing countries could not service their debts. In country after developing country, the IMF and the World Bank agreed to make more loans only under the condition that these countries agree to economic restructuring.

It is this restructuring that is often referred to as the Washington Consensus, the globalization project, and in Latin America as neoliberalism.[8] Like the "trickle down" notion of earlier modernization and development models, neoliberalism and economic restructuring, with their emphasis on "macroeconomic discipline, trade-openness, and market-friendly microeconomic politics" (Williamson 2000, 251), were supposed to help industry, trade, and the economies of rich and poor countries alike. Williamson initially saw the policies he advocated as promoting a more equitable distribution of income and rapid income growth but later acknowledged the importance of how they were implemented as well.

The globalization project began with economic restructuring— downsizing of industry, a shift to offshore production, and the casualization of labor—in the United States in the early 1970s when the postwar boom ceased. Despite the gains that capitalism and especially capitalists in the United States had experienced from development in Mexico and elsewhere, declining profits, largely from internal market saturation and increased international competition led many U.S. corporations to restructure, usually by closing and/or downsizing their facilities. This was often accompanied by a relocation of production to less developed countries and the casualization or flexibilization of labor, involving more part-time employment and subcontracting in both Northern and Southern countries. Among the consequences of this restructuring was a decline in male wages and benefits, increased labor force participation of women, often without benefits, and an increasing gap between the rich and the poor.

In the United States and other advanced capitalist countries such as Great Britain, the impetus for restructuring came from within: from corporations, conservative politicians, and conservative voters.[9] In the developing world, support came from some national elites, but it was pressure from the advanced capitalist countries directly or indirectly via the International Monetary Fund and World Bank that led to the shift to what in Latin America is usually referred to as neoliberalism.

The effects of economic restructuring or neoliberalism in Mexico, as elsewhere, have been enormous. The policy that had prevailed for almost forty years, until the 1980s, and that was in accordance with the approach advanced at the international conference at Bretton Woods in 1944, which emphasized state intervention, the priority of the internal market, and import substitution industrialization, was changed. The new policy, favoring export promotion, called for the state to adopt a strategy of laissez faire as well as financial and market deregulation. The new export-oriented and free market policy has had profound consequences on relations between Mexico and other countries, especially in terms of trade and investment. The opening up of Mexico to international capital and production for export has meant, for example, that Mexico is much more vulnerable to the fluctuations in the economy of the United States, its major trade partner. This greater integration of Mexico into the global economy has, in turn, impacted relations within Mexico. Jorge Castañeda, the former foreign minister who had considered running for the Mexican presidency in 2006, claims that Mexico has lost half a million manufacturing jobs largely to India and China (Friedman 2004). In some areas, such as in the southern state of Chiapas, global integration has prompted rebellion. Elsewhere, including in San Cosme, it has led to more covert forms of resistance and everyday struggle.

To understand the significance of neoliberalism, it is important to note that export promotion, the term commonly used to refer to the current strategy in Mexico and elsewhere in the developing world, is misleading. Mexico (like other colonized areas) has been exporting at least since the Spanish Conquest. What has changed is that whereas raw materials once accounted for most exports, manufacturing of finished products to be consumed elsewhere is now a much greater share of them. In 1980, 10.2 percent of Mexico's total exports were manufactures; by 1994, that figure had grown to 77.4 percent (Dicken 1998, Table 2.6).

Much of this manufacturing for export involves foreign investment, which has increased, especially through transnational corporations, to such an extent that foreign firms accounted for 48 percent of total exports in 1993 and 56 percent in 1996 (Dussel Peters 1998, 10). Foreign ownership of the largest companies has also increased. Between 1993 and 1997, foreign investors increased their percentage of stock in the largest five hundred companies from 10 to 20.4 percent (Tanski & French 2001, 9). Between 1994 and 2002, foreign investment averaged $14 billion a year, up from $700 million in the previous eight years (Lyons 2003). Even with a contraction recently, Mexico is the fourth-largest recipient of foreign investment among developing countries (Kurtenbach 2003). In addition, foreign investment increasingly characterizes the industrial and the financial sectors. Privatization of the banks in 1991 has increased the role of foreign financial resources. Of the eight institutions with nationwide coverage that made up the core of the banking system in 1999, five were Mexican of which two had a minority of foreign participation, and three were foreign (Tanski & French 2001, 100). In 2001, Citigroup acquired Banamex, so foreigners now control about 80 percent of the banking industry. Furthermore, three groups (Citigroup, Banco Bilbao Vizcaya Argentarias, and Banco Santander), all foreign-owned, hold about two-thirds of Mexico's bank deposits (U.S. Dept. of State, Bureau of Economic and Business Affairs 2002, 5).

Global integration has not only meant that the flow of capital into Mexico increased but that Mexican capital now also flows to developed countries not as capital in flight (as was true during the crisis) but for investment (Pozas 1993, 83). Liberalization has thus increased the flow of capital into and out of Mexico along with the increased flow of manufactured exports.

How has Mexico's increased global integration affected different segments and classes of the Mexican population?

The freer flow of capital and goods through neoliberalism, the increasing role of multinational corporations, and the supposedly laissez-faire policies of the state have led some analysts to suggest that under neoliberalism or globalization the nation-state is becoming less important. Many recent discussions of structural adjustment stress the weakness and the withering of the power of the nation-state to make policy decisions for itself compared with the increasing powers of global institutions, transnational processes, and the global market. What these discussions often neglect is the important and increasing role the state plays directly in encouraging capital accumulation and indirectly in increasing inequality. As Harvey notes, behind the facade of a free market, the state plays a different but very important role:

> Contrary to popular belief, market processes do not lead to a "hollowing out" of the state. They entail a deepening of the State's grasp

over certain facets of the social process even as it is driven away from performing some of its more traditional and populist functions. (2000, 180)

Harvey points to the use of state powers to control labor and the increasing militarization of many contemporary nation-states.[10] Contrary to those, such as Appadurai, who see "globalization as a definite marker of a new crisis for the sovereignty of nation states" (1999, 229), Gill (1999), Harvey and others suggest that recent changes in nation-states do not diminish the state's power so much as reorganize it and change who benefits.

As indicated above, during the post–World War II development period, the Mexican state pursued policies that favored industrialization and commercial agriculture over small-scale cultivation. Mexican industrialists and agribusiness interests clearly benefited. *Campesinos* were abandoned by the state, but industrial workers (including many who had been *campesinos*) and a growing middle class gained some benefits from industrial growth, the improvement of public education, and the expansion of public sector employment, especially in health and education.[11] Today, workers and the middle class have also been abandoned, along with small-scale cultivators. The austerity policies of economic restructuring required cutbacks in public social expenditure. Education and health care for the masses have suffered. Capitalists, including international capitalists, however, have benefited from policies ranging from the privatization of state enterprises to the disciplining of labor.

The Mexican state no longer plays a direct role in encouraging industrialization via state enterprises. Now the state indirectly helps the accumulation of private capital by creating favorable conditions for investment (de la Garza Toledo 1993). An example of the state's role in capital accumulation in the private sector is evident in the extensive privatization of state enterprises and in the identity of those who benefited from that privatization. Of the approximately fourteen hundred state enterprises in Mexico in 1983, only two hundred remained in 1993. Carlos Slim, a Mexican entrepreneur who occupied fourth place in a list published by *Forbes* in 1992 of personal fortunes in the world, tripled his fortune from $2.1 million in 1992 to $6.6 million. A good part of it came from his ownership of Teléfonos de México, which was privatized in 1990 (García Villanueva & Stoll 1995, 215, 224).

A recent study also found that Mexico's privatization strengthened the market power of the already large domestic or transnational corporations. The ninety-six companies that were privatized between 1982 and 1991 were sold to only seventeen individuals and enterprises. According to the authors of that study, many "of the government companies were sold to friends of government leaders at relatively low prices" (Tanski & French 2001, 13).

María de los Ángeles Pozas, the author of an important study of the industrial restructuring of Mexican domestic industry, reaches a similar conclusion about the state's role in encouraging the accumulation of private capital. She argues that rather than a "slimming of the Mexican state," there has been "a new type of intervention involving a new alliance between capital and the state" (1993, 85). She points out that the state has supported the private export sector by controlling wages, prices, and interest rates. She stresses also that the state's control of labor is an important factor in the success of the export sector. Cypher suggests that implementing the export promotion policy, like the earlier ISI development project, "required massive state intervention" (1990, 182). Despite state support, however, "the beneficiaries [of export promotion] were an exceedingly small band of national groups and transnational corporations" (Cypher 1990, 183). Only those companies that could make the shift to export promotion benefited from the state's promotional support (Pozas 1993). Furthermore, the number of national companies that have benefited is very small compared with international firms. Excluding Pemex and its subsidiaries, of the hundred principal importers and exporters in 2002, only five were Mexican (Zúñiga 2003).

The neoliberal Mexican state has thus provided the way for greater accumulation of wealth among the haves (in Mexico and elsewhere). It is not surprising, therefore, that although Mexican exports and gross domestic product have been increasing and the deepening of poverty that occurred during what is often referred to as the lost decade has been reduced somewhat, many analysts agree that inequality in Mexico has increased.[12] Recent analyses have found that 43 percent of the population were living in extreme or intermediate poverty in 1999 (Banamex 1999 cited by Tanski & French 2001). As Dussel Peters concludes in his analysis of ten years of the effects of liberalization in Mexico from 1988 to 1997:

> The country's economy is now characterized by an increasing economic polarization, by social exclusion, and by an overwhelming concentration of the GDP and exports within only a few branches of the

economy [automobiles, basic petrochemicals, beer and malt, glass and electronic equipment]. (1998, 11)

Not unlike the dependent development of the Mexican miracle, many of the benefits of Mexico's current growth are also transferred (through profits on foreign investment, technology purchases, foreign debts and trade imbalances) to the wealthy outside of Mexico, especially in the United States. What remains in Mexico goes increasingly to the elite, especially those who are oriented more globally. Rising inequality characterizes all of Latin America, but since 1980 Mexico has had the greatest increase in inequality (Korzeniewich & Smith 2000, 15). The rich in Mexico are significantly richer than they were before economic restructuring, and relatively and absolutely more Mexicans are living in poverty today than in the late 1970s (Polarski 2003). For the vast majority of the Mexican population, neoliberalism has not meant gains.

Neoliberalism in San Cosme: The 1980s

The crisis of the 1980s and consequent restructuring led to high inflation, unemployment, declining formal employment and declining real wages in San Cosme as well as elsewhere in Mexico. San Cosme was especially affected by the large decline in the national textile industry, which could not compete with foreign imports. The liberalization of trade led to the closure of 80 percent of Mexican textile firms and the loss of more than one hundred thousand jobs between 1982 and 1994.[13] The proportion of San Cosme men in factory work declined from almost half of those economically active in 1980 to 29 percent in 1994 (Rothstein 2000, 4).

To deal with job loss, declining wages, and insecurity (even among those who kept their jobs), people in San Cosme turned to a greater reliance on multiple livelihood strategies involving more dependence on the products they themselves produced and increasing the number of wage earners and income generators in a household.[14] Although these strategies sometimes involved activities outside the community, the 1980s was largely a period of retreat within the community. People huddled in larger households to reduce costs. They intensified their subsistence agricultural activities and cut back on expenditures on purchased household items. For example, families that had begun using gas for fuel went back to wood that could be collected locally. They also cut out purchased foods, such as packaged bread and bottled soda, and relied more on what they themselves produced and/or processed, such as tortillas and fruit drinks. Households also increased their reliance on the wage work and income generation of women and youth.

An important exception to the more local and inward orientation that prevailed in the 1980s was increased women's employment in regional factories. During the 1980s, with the encouragement of the state governments of Tlaxcala and Puebla and the national government, export manufacturing, much of it in multinationally owned firms, began to appear in the region. These factories marked the entrance of a beginning stage that in the 1990s became a more significant pattern of foreign-owned factories that employed primarily young women.

To understand the growth of regional employment for women it is necessary to look at the growth of *maquiladoras* in Mexico in general. Especially in the last two decades of the twentieth century, Mexico experienced enormous growth in manufacturing; components (mostly for electronic items and apparel) were imported duty-free into Mexico where they were assembled for export.[15] In the 1970s when *maquiladora* production began, most in-bond assembly production was confined to free trade zones in northern Mexico, and the assembled products were sold only outside Mexico, usually in the United States. Beginning in 1983, incentives were offered to companies to locate *maquila* production to various interior regions, including Tlaxcala. During the 1980s, the proportion of *maquiladoras* in the interior doubled from 10 percent in 1979 to 21 percent in 1989 (Wilson 1992, Table 11). NAFTA broadened further the geographical distribution of *maquiladora* production throughout Mexico, opened up possibilities for the assembly of a wider range of products, and allowed for the sale of more Mexican production in Mexico. The *maquila* sector grew rapidly in the 1990s with over four hundred thousand *maquila* jobs added between 1994 and 1998 and a major export boom following the devaluation of the peso in 1995 (Bair & Gereffi 2001).

A few *maquiladoras* appeared in Tlaxcala in the 1970s as exceptions to the pattern of restricting them to the border zone. They grew in the 1980s and 1990s.[16] Like *maquiladoras* elsewhere, especially in the apparel and electronics sectors, many in Tlaxcala hired women primarily. Despite this growth in regional employment, however, most women and men in San Cosme turned inward: to their families, their subsistence plots, and informal activities within the community to survive the economic crisis.

An important economic activity that emerged at the end of the 1980s, involving a combination of inward and outward orientations (and often relying on experience in textile or garment factories elsewhere), was the production and/or sale of clothing. In one case, for example, two women purchased clothing in the market in Puebla and then resold it in regional markets. Then they decided to make clothing for sale on home sewing machines. In another, a man who feared that he would lose his textile factory job in Mexico City learned to use a sewing machine. He subsequently taught his wife to sew, and he and his wife made girls' dresses that they sold at regional markets. Today, hundreds of households in San Cosme have small workshops or *talleres* where they manufacture clothing. An individual or a family may have two machines on which to sew the cut pieces that are brought to them by a local contractor or a family may employ over forty workers (involving some family members but relying also on wage workers) who sometimes themselves subcontract piecework. These larger workshops engage in every stage, from producing or buying the fabric, deciding on styles and making the patterns, cutting the fabric, assembling the garments, and selling the finished products to middlemen at weekly markets or to those who come to the community to buy for Mexican retailers. San Cosme's garment production, which is mostly for the national market, is a product of both the decline of the previous ISI development strategy and the rise of the new neoliberal strategy. The decline of the ISI strategy reduced formal employment in the textile sector and also adversely affected Mexico's national apparel industry; thus, as we will see in Chapter 4, it opened up possibilities for small-scale garment production in low-wage regions.

As the viability of small-scale agriculture and formal sector employment decreased, people in San Cosme, like people in many other parts of the neoliberalizing world, turned to informal sector employment. A great deal of research throughout the world has shown an increase in informal sector activity since 1980. Why people entered the informal sector also changed during this period. From 1940 to 1980, people entered the informal sector because the formal sector could not absorb them. More recently, however, while many people continue to enter the informal sector for this reason, a pattern has emerged of increasing informalization replacing formal employment. As Castells and Portes (1989, 23) point out, "What is new in the current context is that the informal sector grows, at the expense of already formalized work relationships." Now, many San Cosmeros/as often enter small-scale local garment production even if the possibility of formal employment exists. The insecurity that has been generated by the loss of so many national textile industry jobs has contributed to this shift from formal to informal work.

Additionally, as many commentators have pointed out, not only were many formal sector jobs eliminated by neoliberalism when national industries, such as textiles, could not compete with international competition and when austerity measures cut government jobs, but formal employment has also deteriorated significantly since the early 1980s.[17] For those still employed in the formal sector, inflation and wage controls have cut earnings while attacks on labor have made labor organizing less effective. Consequently, informal sector employment is often seen as more attractive. Much of San Cosme's growth in informal sector participation is in nonmanufacturing services, such as vending foodstuffs, but the major shift into the informal sector has occurred in the garment sector as people have become producers, contractors, and/or merchants. Informal-sector garment production especially became so popular in San Cosme by the mid-1990s that a noticeable change took place, moving people away from education and professional career aspirations for the community's youth to a hope of mobility through economic success in garment manufacturing (Rothstein 1996).

Whether such mobility is probable or even possible, however, depends on the market for locally produced garments. Although San Cosmeros/as produce primarily for the Mexican national market, their share of that market depends on who else is producing for the same market. As more San Cosmeros/as and neighbors from other communities got into the garment business, local competition increased. Trade liberalization means more competition from foreign producers and retailers, such as Wal-Mart, for the same markets. Growing competition for foreign markets and competition within Mexico from its opening to imports from China when China entered the World Trade Organization in 2001 have already raised what people in Mexico refer to as the "China threat" (Jordan 2003). San Cosmeros/as are already producing cheaply and constantly innovating with new and different garments. Whether they can continue to compete against merchants like Wal-Mart, which has the resources to relocate for cheaper production or to use their greater buying power to pressure producers to produce more cheaply, remains to be seen.

Despite the shift from work outside to inside the community, the world is present in San Cosme as never before. Not only is concern with competition from elsewhere a constant pressure and a frequent topic of conversation, but capital, commodities, images, and people flow into the community in unprecedented ways. In a small store on the plaza, Asian-made *chatarra* are sold to local residents that depict the Twin Towers of the World Trade Center, the White House, and the Statue of Liberty.[18]

Contrary to tradition, a number of people now live in the community who were neither born in San Cosme nor are married to someone from San Cosme. One family, connected to San Cosme through their textile business, recently moved to the community and opened a hotel. Professionals from elsewhere have come to live and establish medical and dental practices. Sons and daughters who moved away from San Cosme in the 1960s or whose parents moved elsewhere have now returned to establish businesses or provide professional services. A family left the urban pollution and crowding in the city of Puebla and opened a store selling roast chicken. In 1999, after torrential rains caused flooding and mudslides in the Sierra Norte of Puebla, destroying their homes and villages, a number of Poblanos/as came to San Cosme to live and work. Merchants come, sometimes in droves, to buy the garments produced in San Cosme. Other merchants come to sell garments, DVDs, household items, and many other things at the three weekly markets that now take place in the community. Workers from poorer neighboring villages come to work in the garment workshops.

As consumption and consumerism have grown, especially among the many young people in the community who now have some disposable income from their employment in the garment workshops, more outsiders as well as insiders are opening stores selling furniture, clothing, and Internet service or performing services as doctors, dentists, exercise teachers, or shoemakers for the residents of San Cosme. The flow of people, images, ideas, and commodities into the community is unparalleled.

The flow of things, people, and ideas out of the community is also more diverse than ever. Whereas men left the community in the 1950s, 1960s, and 1970s for factory work, women, men, and children leave for a variety of reasons today. Travel to other towns and cities has become much easier. A road built in the late 1970s provides a more direct route between Puebla and Santa Ana, an important commercial town to the west. Buses pass along the road every few minutes. Other buses, taxis, and privately owned cars run from almost all corners of San Cosme to different cities and towns in Tlaxcala as well as to Puebla. Many residents of San Cosme have been to the United States, to different areas of

Mexico, to Cuba, and elsewhere to work or visit. Along with the flow of people flow ideas. A group of San Cosmeros/as went to the American Southwest to demonstrate Carnival dancing at a museum. Recipes from San Cosme's kitchens appear in a collection of regional recipes published by the Museum of Popular Arts and Traditions in Tlaxcala.

In today's world, people and things move with unprecedented velocity, and even within relatively stable communities "the warp of these stabilities is everywhere shot through with the woof of human motion" (Appadurai 1990, 7). Even those who rarely leave the community have children, grandchildren, and other relatives living elsewhere in Mexico or in the United States with whom they speak by telephone and from whom they receive remittances. Doña María cares for her five-year-old great granddaughter whose parents are living in the United States. During a recent telephone conversation, the girl's mother criticized the way Doña María had dressed the girl to go to school; apparently, someone had reported to the mother that the girl was not dressed well. Many San Cosmeros/as explicitly point to their new dependence on markets, remittances, jobs, and other influences from elsewhere. Some discuss these influences in analytic terms, using concepts like imperialism or globalization. Whether or not they leave the community often or discuss the causes of the changes they experience, their greater awareness of their own vulnerability corresponds to the greater flux in their lives.

What has most profoundly transformed San Cosme and many other similar communities, however, is not what flows into and out of the community but what underlies it; that is, the flexible accumulation and capital mobility that makes people's positions very precarious and makes the influence of external forces more pervasive. People from San Cosme who went temporarily—usually weekly—to live and work in Mexico City usually brought their local ideas about kinship, religion, and political patterns with them. Although they returned to San Cosme with new resources, ideas, and social and political relations that affected the community in numerous ways, they melded the old and the new into hybrid patterns in which the local predominated. They produced an indigenized modernity. They brought their political contacts, for example, back home to be used to build local schools. They used new social ties with outsiders, such as *compadres* who lived in Mexico City, to provide housing so that a son or daughter could get the higher education available in the city but still not readily available nearby. They brought the outside in.

Today, global forces prevail in a new and different way. In the next chapter I show how San Cosme changed from a peasant to a proletarian community in the 1950s and 1960s and then became increasingly involved with flexible garment production. I suggest that flexible garment production may be a temporary occurrence but that many of the changes with which it is associated (as we will see in subsequent chapters) are likely to have effects that endure.

CHAPTER 3

From Peasants to Worker-Peasants
to Small-Scale Flexible Producers

Don Juan Sánchez[1] is a fifty-five-year-old *campesino* and one of the few men in San Cosme who has never been a factory worker. An only son, he and his wife, Doña Mercedes, inherited their house and about three hectares of land from his parents and three hectares of land from her parents. For many years while his mother was alive, they worked her three hectares as well as their own land. His mother, along with Don Juan, Doña Mercedes, and their four children, lived primarily off the production of their land. Their subsistence was supplemented by the sale of some corn, the occasional sale of animals they raised, by working for wages on land belonging to others, and, until the 1980s, by occasional nonagricultural wage labor. As a consequence of his active participation in the National Peasant Confederation (CNC) in the late 1970s, he and several other *campesinos* were able to buy a tractor that they rent out to further supplement their families' incomes. In the 1980s he began working as a mason, and his wife began selling prepared food in the afternoons in Puebla. Like others who managed to continue as *campesinos/as* for most of their lives, they have been able to support themselves primarily from their agricultural activities by supplementing them with a variety of part-time and sporadic jobs.

Until the 1940s, all the residents of San Cosme were *campesinos/ as* (agricultural smallholders) in what can best be described as a family economy. Families produced primarily for their own subsistence on land they owned or expected to inherit. Although some people were also part-time specialists, such as musicians, masons, barbers, or storekeepers, agriculture was everyone's main source of livelihood. By 1980, less than one of every four households continued to rely primarily on what they themselves produced. Today, although many families continue to cultivate corn, very few households rely primarily on their own subsistence production.[2] Most *campesinos/as'* households receive pensions or remittances from sons and daughters elsewhere.[3] Don Juan and Doña Mercedes still call themselves *campesinos/as*, but their married son, married daughter, and their spouses live with them. Both the son and the son-in-law work full time in a garment workshop, and the household's income is primarily from nonagricultural sources.

People now rely on a wide variety of new, modern economic activities, including professions such as medicine, teaching, dentistry, and architecture; commercial and entrepreneurial efforts, such as a *farmacia* that sells prescription and over-the-counter drugs as well as personal care products and gifts, or an Internet cafe or video rental store; and many garment-related activities, ranging from manufacture or contracting to textile making or operating a store selling thread, trimmings, and/or fabrics. How San Cosme changed from subsistence production to a more modern economy is the subject of this chapter. It is a story of hard work, creativity, and struggle against disadvantage.

San Cosme's Family Economy

Until the 1940s, even with low productivity from poor-quality land and agriculture dependent upon rainfall, the residents of San Cosme had enough land to provide for their families. Most people planted corn, squash, and beans using the traditional plow culture (oxen drawing a wooden implement). Most families also relied on fruit and vegetables, such as *nopales* (prickly pears), which they grew in gardens near their houses. People also raised pigs and/or chickens for their own consumption and for sale and had donkeys, horses, or mules for transporting corn and other products to and from their fields.

Campesino households supplemented their agriculture with a variety of cash-generating activities to cover expenses for clothing, household items, as well as religious and school costs. They sometimes worked for wages on someone else's lands, usually that of a factory worker from the neighboring community of Papalotla. As more men from San Cosme themselves became factory workers, *campesinos* increasingly worked on the land of their neighbors in San Cosme. Some also made and sold *pulque* (an alcoholic drink made from the maguey plant) or charcoal or sold wood that they gathered from the mountain for fuel.

Over the years, some *campesinos/as* experimented with various new technologies but, given the temporal nature of cultivation, the small and diminishing size of landholdings, and the poor soil quality, even the use of chemical fertilizers, some use of tractors, and motorized transport have not increased productivity. The soil deteriorated further, and San Cosmeros/as lost land to roads, housing, schools, and other public spaces, and other resources such as wood, wild animals, and wild mushrooms disappeared. Each year, as the population grew unaccompanied by any change in the method of agriculture that would increase productivity, more people lacked the amount of land necessary for subsistence.[4] Today, most families plant only some corn, and increasingly, as the price of corn declines more and more, not even corn is planted and lands are left uncultivated or turned into housing sites.[5] Even for the many who rely on their own corn production for tortillas, the family economy that once existed is gone, and the corn they grow is at most a supplement to income generated through the market in labor or products.

The Family and the Family Economy

A family economy meant not only that people relied primarily on their own production, but that the unit of production, reproduction, and consumption was the same. Work on the land was done by the members of the family for the family. When additional labor was needed, family members exchanged labor with kin or neighbors. Everyone in the family, young and old, male and female, participated in the labor of the household, including agricultural and domestic tasks.

For most people, the nuclear family was the basic unit; that is, only within it were obligations and responsibilities binding. Most people lived in nuclear households, but even in extended households (29 percent in 1971), coresidence did not necessarily mean cooperation. Only when older members used their ownership of land to control younger members through the promise of inheritance rights or the threat of their revocation did cooperation involve the whole household.

Although the nuclear family was the important unit, it was always embedded in a broader web of kin relations. There were few binding obligations with regard to other kin, but the kindred—that is, relatives traced through both males or females and through marriage—was an important resource from which people drew support. As I have indicated, kin frequently relied on each other for exchange labor in their

Figure 3.1. Feeding chickens, 1980

fields. Kin also provided domestic labor and loans of cash or goods. They frequently shared food. When people brought a gift to a fiesta and/or if they were kin, they were given *mole* (the traditional dish served at fiestas) to take home. To this day, when anyone receives *mole*, he or she then shares it with their family, often including those who do not live in the same household. People often receive large portions if they are godparents, have high status, and/or have given a gener- ous gift. The redistribution of *mole*, which includes chicken, turkey, or pork, is an important source of meat in many families. Agricultural products were and continue to be regularly shared. When someone comes back from the fields or the mountain with *caña* (cornstalks that are chewed like sugarcane), squash, *capulín* (wild cherries) or *tejocotes* (a wild fruit), what they have returned with is distributed to various family members, such as siblings in other households. Similarly, people usually cut some corn before it is dry and ready to be used for corn dough as in tortillas or to be boiled or roasted on the cob or made into *chilatole* (a corn soup). These, too, are often shared among family members in other households.

Although kinship in San Cosme was (and still is) flexible in the sense that some relations are not necessarily characterized by particular obligations, cultural rules specified that, for life cycle events and religious rituals, closer kin (usually the parents and siblings of the couple making the event) should help in the preparations and that more distant kin (usually through second cousins or three ascending generations through both males and females as well as ritual kin) should be invited. Getting together assured that people knew their kin and knew also how they might be expected to be of help.[6] In addition, the obligations to members of one's nuclear family of orientation carried into adulthood so that there was a great deal of sharing among adult siblings and between adult sons and daughters and their parents, even when they were no longer living together. Since most house sites were inherited, kin often lived at the same address or at adjacent addresses in a pattern that Blim (1990) calls "modified extensionality." Proximity facilitated sharing labor, information, and goods.

When I went to San Cosme in 1971, agriculture was still the main source of income for more than half of the economically active population, and most households still relied primarily or heavily on it. Although the influence of factory work and factory workers was increasing, the family economy was still strong. Even if they worked in Mexico City (sixty miles away), factory workers were oriented to their home community and the agricultural way of life. Most workers had gone to work in the factories because they did not have enough land for subsistence. With their first factory earnings they often purchased additional land so that they had enough to provide corn for tortillas for their families. Many workers quit their factory jobs and returned to life as *campesinos* after working in a factory for a few years. A growing number of differences between *campesinos* and factory workers, however, underscored the distinctive characteristics of the family economy and the changes brought about by proletarianization.

Campesino households, for example, were characterized by more egalitarian relations between women and men. The older generation often had greater authority than younger family members, and reciprocity and nonmarket relations were more significant. Social relations among *campesinos/as* were also more bounded by the community than those between factory workers and their families, who were developing patterns of dependence of women on men, of old on young, and on relations with fellow workers, bosses, union leaders, politicians, and other people and institutions beyond the community. Those patterns would eventually dominate the community, but in the early 1970s it was still possible to observe a different structure of dependence in the family economy.

Gender and Age in the Family Economy

As I have indicated above, in the *campesino* family economy everyone was involved in production. Furthermore, production and consumption were part of a continuum. Women and men of all ages participated in planting and harvesting. For corn, the major crop, men and older boys usually performed the tasks that involved animals—plowing, loading, and transporting. Women and children planted and women cut the points of the corn to hasten the drying process and cut the corn and *zacate* (dried cornstalks used for fodder and fuel). After the corn was harvested, it was removed from the cob to be stored. Women spent more time shucking corn than did men, but men and children over the age of six, as well as women, usually participated. Once it was shucked, women and girls were responsible for most of the cooking and serving of the corn, mainly in the form of tortillas.[7]

Overlapping spheres for women and men also characterized animal raising. Women and girls cared for the chickens and turkeys, and women usually slaughtered them. Men and boys fed pigs, cows, and horses and cleaned pigpens. Men slaughtered pigs and cows. Women or men cared for goats and sheep. Both men and women also participated in various economic activities to generate supplementary cash income.

These relationships can be illustrated with a typical case, that of Don Luis and Doña Marta. They lived with his mother and had two and a half hectares which, along with a herd of sheep and goats ranging from ten to fifty animals (cared for by the mother), provided most of the support for the household of three adults and two children. They sold about a thousand kilos of corn a year (at about one peso a kilo[8]) and some sheep and goats. Don Luis also worked for wages on other people's land about thirty days a year and worked on an alfalfa truck that came to the community a few hours a week. Doña Marta worked for wages on other people's land about twenty days a year and earned

Figure 3.2. Man who called himself "Un verdadero campesino"
(a true *campesino*), 2005

one or two pesos a day selling eggs from her house from the chickens
she raised.

Men assumed the greatest responsibility for decision making about
cash and farming, but women had significant roles in production. In
spot observations done in 1980, women did less agricultural and more
domestic work than men, but in only one of eight *campesino* families was
all the agricultural work done by men.[9] Income generation by women

or men was sporadic and intermittent, and the cash generated by any one member of the household was not the sole or primary basis of family support.

Age, rather than gender, was associated with dominance. Older men and older women usually retained control of land that would be inherited by their sons and daughters when the parents died. Adult sons and daughters usually had use of a parcel of land that they would later inherit, but the older generation retained control and they could use that control to dominate younger family members. Older men often assigned men's tasks to younger men; older women organized domestic labor and delegated responsibility to younger women for agricultural tasks. Doña Alberta recalled that when she was first married, her mother-in-law, with whom she lived, sent her out to the fields every day while the mother-in-law stayed home and socialized with her friends. Another woman talked about how her mother-in-law, who thought the daughter-in-law had induced an abortion, threatened to cut off their inheritance if she tried to abort again.

Until 1943, when factory workers from San Cosme gained control of local politics and San Cosme was made an independent municipality, local politics was dominated by factory workers and union leaders from San Francisco Papalotla, the headtown of the municipality of which San Cosme was part. Within San Cosme, the religious hierarchy established prestige and influence. Here, as in other aspects of the family economy, elders dominated. Although men had the public positions, it was the family that enabled a man to sponsor a saint and thus move up the social ladder. A man whose family, including the women and especially the wife, did not want to participate would be unable to have the necessary fiestas and celebrations.[10]

Since men and women inherited land equally and both participated in agriculture and other sporadic income-generating activities, women were not any more economically dependent on men than men were on them. The bulk of a family's consumption came from its own production. Although market participation enabled a family to buy goods it did not produce and to get the cash to do so, nonmarket economics was the rule and was characterized by reciprocity. Labor was donated as part of a generalized reciprocal relationship. A son, for example, worked on his parents' land, or siblings worked on each other's plots. Services were often exchanged for goods. In return for doing the laundry and going to the mill for her aunt's mother-in-law, a thirteen-year-old girl received shoes, food, and other items.

A heavy reliance on nonmarket activity does not necessarily imply either that it is not exploitative or that it levels economic differences.[11] As Dow (1977, 222) points out about the *cargo* system among the Otomí, redistribution can convert wealth into prestige and authority. *Cargo* holders in San Cosme, as elsewhere, received prestige. It is worth repeating that redistribution of food at fiestas was an important pattern of exchange in the family economy. Although the pattern of distribution was influenced heavily by kinship, the prestige of the guest and the gift, if any, that the guest brought were also important. Consequently, wealthier and/or more prestigious guests were put in a position of having more food to distribute to others. It is important to note, however, that even the wealthiest households could not use their wealth to generate much more wealth or power. Given the nature of the land, more of it did not yield much profit. One could earn interest in money lending or invest in a mill or a general store, but the limited cash income of everyone in the community restricted profits. Furthermore, until the 1940s when San Cosme was still part of the municipality of San Francisco, politics was dominated by residents of the head-town, and no one in San Cosme, including the highest *cargo* holders, had much political authority. Not until San Cosmeros became factory workers were they able to gain some control over local politics and decide local issues such as the building of roads and schools.

Relations Within and Beyond the Community

When I went to San Cosme in 1971, there was one unpaved main street that led through Papalotla to the highway to Puebla, then one of Mexico's largest cities. Buses ran between San Cosme's main street and Puebla every forty minutes between 6 a.m and 8:30 p.m. and from Puebla until 12:30 p.m. At the highway, one could also get a bus to the state capital, Tlaxcala. People from San Cosme went to Puebla to work, study, shop, or for recreation and to Tlaxcala mostly for government business. But it was mostly factory workers and their families who traveled to Puebla or Tlaxcala. *Campesinos/as* had fewer reasons to go to Puebla.

The boundedness of *campesino* society was apparent not only in that economic activities were largely confined to San Cosme and Papalotla, the neighboring community, but in that most social relations were similarly within that space. *Compadrazgo*—the system of ritual kin relationships established through participation in Catholic or, for a few families,

Protestant rituals of birth, marriage, and other important events in the life cycle—and marriage were among the most important social relations in the community. Especially in the past, *compadrazgo* relations formalized an existing relationship, for example, between neighbors and established the long-term obligations and responsibilities of godparents to a child or children and between the co-parents. *Campesinos/as* rarely had *compadres* from outside San Cosme, except occasionally from Papalotla, and then usually from Xolalpa, the barrio of Papalotla that borders San Cosme. Proletarian families had not only more *compadres* from elsewhere, they also developed new and different types of *compadrazgo*.[12] In addition to the intensive relations formed around life-cycle events, workers also sought *padrinos* to sponsor a new house or a new store. Found more often in urban than rural areas of Mexico, these were characterized by less intensive relations between the *compadres*.[13]

Campesinos were also more likely than factory workers to marry women from San Cosme. Of the non-*campesino* men who married civilly in San Cosme in 1971, almost one-third (eleven of thirty-four) married women from elsewhere, usually from neighboring communities in Puebla or Tlaxcala whom they had met through fellow workers. None of the eleven *campesino* men who married that year did so.

While the everyday lives of *campesinos/as* and the family economy were bounded by and centered on the community, changing economic and political processes in the region, nation, and the world had already undermined that boundedness. These processes would continue to do so and at a pace that was accelerating.

The Impact of Factory Work

During the Second World War, when the Mexican textile industry grew, some men from San Cosme, usually from families with less land, began working in textile factories in Mexico City or Puebla. As the value of agricultural production declined and land pressure continued to mount, the number of factory workers, especially textile workers, increased. By 1980, more than half of the economically active men were factory workers, and more than three-quarters of the households relied primarily on cash income (Rothstein 1982, 27, 53).

Despite their proletarianization, San Cosme's factory workers maintained strong commitments to the community and to subsistence production. Although most of the *obreros* worked in Mexico City, few moved to the Federal District. Instead, they commuted weekly, often on buses that ran directly to and from San Cosme and the factories that employed the most San Cosmeros. Most factory workers married women from San Cosme. Those who married women from elsewhere brought their wives to live in San Cosme. The workers built houses, participated in local politics, and bought land on which they practiced subsistence cultivation.

Until recently, much of the literature on migration suggested a one-way movement from rural to urban areas.[14] Even studies that recognized that migrants sometimes returned home failed to see them having much of an impact on their home communities.[15] Despite the limitations that migrants face, largely because of the structural inequalities that they and their neighbors in communities such as San Cosme experience, San Cosme's factory workers had an enormous impact on their families, their neighbors, and the community in general. But although they returned to San Cosme daily, weekly, or permanently with many new resources and ideas, such as more cash and values favoring formal education and professional training, and affected the community in numerous ways, they melded the old and the new and the internal and the external together into hybrid patterns in which the local dominated. Many of these continuities, especially the continuation of subsistence cultivation and a flexible kinship system, gave community members an advantage in subsequent decades. As I discuss below, however, not all members of the community had the same advantages. Factory work decreased the distance between San Cosmeros and some outsiders, such as the residents of Papalotla. But factory work also increased the gap in economic control and decision making between women and men and thereby contributed to growing gender inequality. Eventually also, factory work enabled the *obreros* to take control over local politics. Thus, the social distance between *campesinos* and *obreros* increased.

Factory Work and Family Life

In the family economy, as indicated above, relations between women and men were relatively egalitarian. An important factor contributing to that equality was women's highly valued role in agriculture and domestic work. In 1971, a *campesina* I asked about her occupation responded with a long list of activities, including work in the fields, laundry, getting wood, caring for animals, cooking, and many others. In just a few years, however, women's work became devalued. In 1974, a woman in San Cosme I asked why she thought the neighboring community was more modern said it was because the women of Papalotla stayed home and took care of their families. They did not go out to work in the fields. In that year also, young women in proletarian households who were no longer in school were described as doing nothing. By 1980, most proletarian women in San Cosme stayed home. While their husbands and hired workers harvested corn (the major agricultural activity), wives prepared the meal that the field-workers would eat when they were finished for the day.[16]

Proletarian women were also more likely to have gas stoves, beds rather than *petates* (straw sleeping mats), televisions, and houses made of cement rather than adobe. By then also, almost everybody had electricity and potable water. There is no doubt that these modern conveniences often make women's work easier. As studies of women's work in the United States early in the twentieth century show, however, these new, so-called conveniences come with costs for their users.

First, they require cash purchases and thus make those without access to cash more dependent on those with access—in this case, women on men. Proletarian women's retreat from agriculture was related to the declining value of subsistence production. Although proletarian families continued to practice subsistence farming, the lowering of the productivity of their land and of the price of corn increasingly reduced its value. Consequently, proletarians began practicing a less intensive form of agriculture: instead of planting squash, beans, and corn, only corn was planted and less time spent weeding. Whereas *campesinos/as* would cut *elotes* (corn on the cob) or cane before the corn was dry enough to make flour for tortillas, proletarians went to the fields only for the final harvest. Proletarian men continued to participate in their own harvest on their days off, but they, like women and children, found other ways of spending their time. But whereas men replaced agricultural work with paid work, women replaced it with unpaid domestic work. There were few paid work alternatives for women. The jobs men had were not open to them. If women had to earn cash, they worked in the fields for others or as maids. Given the nature of their alternatives, women did not work outside the home unless they had to.

Women whose husbands were factory workers became dependent on their husbands for cash and for the gas stoves, blenders, refrigerators, and other household items that made their lives easier. To this day, few families have washing machines because women's labor has been devalued and because women with less education lack opportunities, so that one can hire a woman or a girl to do the washing very cheaply. Women's dependence on men means also that some women stayed with husbands whom they otherwise might have left. In one case, a woman separated from her factory worker husband because he had a girlfriend. After leaving her children with her mother and working as a maid in Mexico City for a few years, she decided to go back with her husband. Even though he spent most of his time with the other woman, she and her children moved back into their house. He regularly provided her with some cash, and she did some domestic chores such as laundry for him.

A second cost involved in the new proletarian homemaker role was the increasing isolation and confinement of women to their houses. *Campesinas* spent time outside their houses when they went to the fields or to the mountain to collect wood or wild vegetables or fruit. Some still went to the stream to wash their clothes. Proletarian women's work no longer entailed going out to the fields or mountain to do agricultural work or to the stream to do the laundry. Furthermore, as male family members increasingly went to factories or participated in politics and children became more involved with school, proletarian women were left without assistance to do their domestic work. As their standard of living elevated, they usually had more clothes and linens to wash, more tile floors to clean, and more diverse meals to cook. Although proletarian women whose husbands worked in Mexico City were likely to live in extended family households and might therefore have some assistance with domestic tasks, when the husband was gone (six out of seven days), the mother-in-law frequently dominated. Among proletarian families in which the husband worked in Puebla and commuted daily, his wages usually allowed a couple and their children to establish an independent household sooner than *campesinos/as* could.[17] Although extended families do not necessarily cooperate, it is more difficult to share domestic tasks in nuclear families. A proletarian woman thus experienced more isolation and subordination—to her husband because of economic dependence and to her mother-in-law if he worked in Mexico City and they lived with his parents.

Although women's work in subsistence cultivation had become devalued and proletarian women more isolated and dependent on their husbands as breadwinners, women were not looked down upon. Men and women were thought to be involved in different spheres of activity; women were in a private sphere of domestic work while men participated in a public world of politics and factory work. In 1982 I wrote:

"The native model does not yet relegate the different spheres of proletarian women and men to different ranks" (Rothstein, 78). But as I will show in Chapter 5, the basis for further deterioration of women's position had been established.

Factory Work and Community Development

Factory work affected not only gender and family relations and families' standards of living, it also improved the community's resources and services and changed relations within it. One of the first efforts by the earliest factory workers was to petition to have San Cosme made an independent municipality. In the early 1940s also, factory workers successfully fought to get the buses that at that time went only as far as Papalotla (a mile away) to continue on past San Cosme's central plaza to the end of the main street. Those efforts, and many that followed, were successful because factory workers used their union contacts in a patron-client system that enabled them to have some access to some of the benefits of Mexico's economic miracle.[18]

Despite rapid economic growth during the post–World War II boom, Mexico's dependent capitalism constrained the way benefits were distributed. Much of the domestically produced surplus was transferred, especially to the United States, to repay foreign debts which had increased significantly to cover infrastructural and other costs involved in import substitution industrialization. Also being paid were foreign investors whose profit grew ten times between 1940 and 1974 (Cockcroft 1990, calculated from Table 3). What remained was very unequally distributed, with the rural population benefiting the least.[19] As many critics have pointed out, productivity, which grew because it was promoted by protected industrialization, was not accompanied by comparable growth in employment because the kind of manufacturing technology that was being transferred from the core was supposedly labor saving, turning those who were fortunate enough to get such jobs into a "worker elite."[20] In 1970 it was estimated that 45 percent of the labor force was underemployed, mostly in the agricultural sector (Gollás & García Rocha 1976, 406). Public sector spending similarly benefited the urban and more affluent over the rural and the poor.

That San Cosme was able to derive some benefits and that at least some individuals were able to experience mobility into this worker elite was unusual. By 1970, using their labor union contacts with the dominant political party, the Partido Revolucionario Institucional (PRI) and government officials, San Cosme's factory workers had acquired electricity and potable water and improved roads and schools for their home community. The state of Tlaxcala initiated a development program to attract foreign capital that contributed to some of the infrastructural improvements, but many of the neighboring communities did not fare as well as San Cosme. Of the eight municipalities in San Cosme's district, only three had potable water, and one of those three had it only in some sections. All eight had electricity, but only parts of the *municipios* were electrified in three of the communities. San Cosme's relative good fortune was due at least in part to its having been pushed into factory work during the period of rapid Mexican economic growth. Although land is relatively equally distributed in Tlaxcala, San Cosme was and is one of the densest communities in the state. Men and women from other communities with more land were able to delay their entry into full-time wage work. By the time they too were pushed into it, however, Mexico's rate of growth had declined and jobs were scarcer.

The greatest gains that San Cosmeros/as made were individual. As Frank suggested more than thirty years ago, the modernization of Mexico in the 1940s, 1950s, and 1960s was not sufficient to provide for much social mobility, but limited opportunities or chances for higher rank did exist for those who played according to the rules of the game (1969, 313). By 1980, San Cosme boasted more schools than surrounding communities, including a kindergarten and a telesecondary school, in which some subjects were taught via television. Many families were able to take advantage of their higher income from factory work and the greater availability of schools to educate their children, particularly their sons, in the hope that they would become professionals. But opportunities were not equal for all.

Proletarian sons were much more likely to be encouraged and allowed to stay in school than daughters. In 1980 more than 60 percent of the sons of factory workers had more than a primary school education compared to only 24 percent of their daughters (Rothstein 1982, Table 20). Sons and daughters from *campesino* families were even less likely to stay in school. Only 19 percent of daughters and 20 percent of sons from *campesino* families had more than primary school. *Campesinos/as* were less likely to have the financial resources that additional schooling required, and many could not afford the loss of labor that it necessitated. Furthermore, since education in San Cosme went only through secondary school, additional schooling (or secondary school that did not rely on television for teaching, which many residents thought was better) required either commuting or staying with kin or friends elsewhere. Given their more bounded social lives, *campesinos/as* were less likely to have the social contacts who could provide housing for their sons or daughters in towns or cities that had better schooling.

Continuities and Similarities

Although differences between *campesinos/as* and proletarians and between the sexes were increasing, many social patterns served to minimize them. Kinship continued to be important. People in San Cosme had a flexible kinship system in which kin provided a network to draw upon for a variety of labor and resource needs. That pattern of relying on kin persisted as the community changed. Proletarian families more often shared their knowledge of and contacts with the outside world, for example, by providing help in getting jobs, schooling, or political support.[21] *Campesino* families shared agricultural products that proletarians no longer grew or collected, such as wild mushrooms, *caña,* or *elotes.* Relations between *campesinos/as* and proletarians became more monetized as workers increasingly hired them to work in their fields or as *albañiles* (masons) to work on their houses. The average factory worker earned twice as much as the average *campesino* (Rothstein 1974, 111), but the availability of factory work throughout the 1960s and most of the 1970s kept the gap from growing.

Even in the early 1970s, few households held anyone who had not been a worker at some time. In a sample of twenty-eight households that had no regular wage or commercial income in 1971, a household member either had been or became a factory worker in more than half of them (fifteen). Eight of the remaining thirteen were either headed by women or by men over the age of sixty who had no adult sons or daughters living with them.

By 1980, only a quarter of San Cosme's households still relied primarily on agriculture, and in many of them someone had worked in a factory at some time. Consequently, except for a few *campesino* households, experience with factory work was common. Furthermore, everyone had a son, son-in-law, brother, brother-in-law, or cousin who had worked in a textile factory. The differences between proletarians and *campesinos/as* thus were quantitative rather than qualitative.

What distinguished factory workers and their families from *campesinos/as* was that the former had more involvement in factory work because more members worked in factories and/or had a longer history of having done so. Although this unequal involvement contributed to greater differences in income and contacts, until the 1980s the opportunities for men to become factory workers were widely available. Since most got their jobs by knowing someone already working in the factory, San Cosmeros had an advantage over the residents of many other communities who had no such connections.

To some extent, the cash that workers brought into the community also provided more local opportunities for others to supplement agriculture with a mill or a general store or with part-time work as musicians or masons. Since all the *campesinos/as* had at least some land and the opportunities for wage work within San Cosme were not sufficient to convert many of them into regular wage laborers for proletarian families, those who did not work in factories were not dependent on those who did. Although there were important differences between proletarians and *campesinos/as,* many *campesinos* had been workers, workers continued to practice agriculture, *campesinos* could almost always get jobs as workers, and there was a "trickle-down" of the higher earnings and community improvements that the politically connected workers had obtained. Thus, the line between workers and *campesinos/as* was fluid rather than fixed and their relations, although at times exploitative, were not those of different classes.

The relatively privileged position of factory workers in Mexico contributed to the gains that San Cosme's proletarians made and to the openness of factory work for *campesinos* during the period of economic growth of the 1960s and early 1970s. But all this was to change drastically during the economic crisis of the 1980s. Most residents of San Cosme, like people throughout the developing world, lost the gains they had made during the postwar boom. In the global economy that has emerged since the 1990s, some San Cosmeros/as have gained, especially as consumers of global commodities. However, as has been true everywhere, the losers outnumber the winners, and the winners in San Cosme now often gain at the expense of the losers. Before they were to make those gains, however, San Cosmeros/as had to deal with *el crisis.*

The Other Side of the Miracle:
Coping with the Crisis and with Losses

During the 1980s, economic growth in Mexico slowed down considerably and at times stopped. As indicated in Chapter 2, to deal with the economic crisis, Mexico restructured its economy along the lines dictated by the IMF, the World Bank, and by the United States through those international agencies. Tariffs on imports and other trade restrictions were reduced and/or eliminated. State enterprises were privatized. Austerity diminished the state's involvement in social expenditures. These efforts restructured the economy to favor export manufacturing built on Mexico's relative advantage of cheap labor. The overall thrust of restructuring was to open the economy to international capital and products and to reduce government spending on services to the poor and working class.

For the residents of San Cosme, restructuring meant inflation, wage controls, and the loss of many factory jobs. As many of Mexico's national textile factories closed or cut back production, the proportion of San Cosme men in factory work, predominantly in textile factories, declined from 48 percent in 1980 to 38 percent in 1989 and to 29 percent in 1994. During the 1980s, because of wage controls and inflation, their real wages, like those of others in Mexico, declined to the level of the mid-1960s (Barkin 1986). Government reductions in health, education, and other services further cut into their standard of living.

As indicated above, although there had been significant changes within households and the community as a result of the movement of men into factory work, most proletarian families continued to cultivate land, and they retained their flexible kinship system. When the crisis occurred, subsistence cultivation and flexible kinship enabled San Cosmeros/as to survive and get past it.

One of the most noticeable changes in the 1980s was a return to greater reliance on subsistence production. Proletarian families that had decreased cultivation by planting only corn went back to planting corn, squash, and beans. Families who had planted corn but had not done much more than plant and harvest now went to their fields more frequently to apply fertilizer, weed, and check on growth in order to increase productivity. That these efforts helped was evident by the fact that out of twenty-seven families interviewed in 1984, more than half (fifteen) said they expected to have enough corn for their families for the coming year. Four said that they would supplement their own production by buying "a little" corn.

Families also decreased the need for cash by relying on small quantities of diverse products they could produce. Whereas in the 1970s a family might harvest only once and then only dry corn (*mazorca*) when the whole field was ready, now they would cut small quantities of *caña* (corncane), *elotes* (ripe but not dry corn for roasting or boiling), squash, squash flowers, or fruit whenever they were ready. They went more often to their fields to get weeds for fodder and fuel. By intensifying their agricultural production and using more products that they themselves produced, by burning weeds instead of petroleum, for example, or by feeding their animals *hierba* (weeds) instead of alfalfa and then eating more tortillas instead of bread, proletarian (or formerly proletarian) families were able to decrease their reliance on purchased items and on cash. People also substituted locally produced and/or other nonindustrial products for manufactured goods. For example, they increased their consumption of lemonade and other fresh or dried fruit drinks instead of bottled soda.

Kinship also helped San Cosmeros survive the crisis. San Cosmeros continued to rely on kin to get jobs, political support, and for agricultural and domestic labor. They also increased their reliance on multiple income-pooling strategies. They did this in two ways. First, more people lived together. In the 1970s, as the wages of workers enabled them to establish independent households sooner than they could have as *campesinos*, the proportion of nuclear family households increased. During the crisis of the 1980s, San Cosmeros/as turned again to extended family households. In the early 1970s, 29 percent of households were extended; by 1989, 44 percent were (Rothstein 1995, Table 7-1). Extended family households not only reduce costs, but huddling increases the number of income generators per household. Nuclear family households averaged 1.2 income generators compared to 1.6 in extended households (Rothstein 1995, 173–174).

The residents of San Cosme also increased the number of income generators per household, doubling them between 1980 and 1994 (Rothstein 1995, Table 1), by increasing the labor force participation and self-employment of women and youth. In the 1970s most women gardened and raised pigs and chickens. *Campesinas* worked in their own fields and sometimes as agricultural laborers, but few women were employed or heavily involved in wage work or commercial activities. By

1989, however, the proportion of women reported as participating in the labor force or in self-employment had nearly doubled—from 9 percent in 1980 to 17 percent in 1989. By 1994, the rate was 37 percent for women twelve and over, and 50 percent among women between fifteen and nineteen. Young men also experienced an increase in paid work, but unlike women who moved into paid work from homemaking, they left studying for paid work (Rothstein 1996, Table 2).

Young men, women, and older men became increasingly involved in the growing, small-scale, flexible garment industry. To understand that industry and how it has come to dominate life and labor in San Cosme, it is necessary to examine flexible garment manufacturing both there and globally.

CHAPTER 4

Flexible Garment Production

Beginning in 1989, *talleres,* or home workshops that manufacture clothing of various sorts, began appearing in San Cosme. Most were started by
former factory workers or by workers who anticipated that their factories
might close. Within ten years, hundreds of workshops were founded by
people with varying work experiences, including former factory workers,
professionals, and *campesinos/as.* The workshops range from households
with two machines, to which cut pieces are delivered by local contractors and sewn by family members, to households with thirty or forty
workers and many different machines, which produce the fabric and garments and sell the finished products either at wholesale to middlemen
or at retail to consumers at weekly markets. Most of the *talleres* are
small, with fewer than five workers, but about twenty larger workshops
employ fifteen or more.

Along with the growth of garment production has come a surge in
related retail activity. A weekly market selling mostly garments to San
Cosmeros/as and people from neighboring communities was established
in San Cosme in the mid-1990s. A number of stores specializing in garments, fabric, and sewing supplies have opened up, and many people
work in the garment trade as brokers or contractors who arrange for
production for others. Men, and sometimes women, from San Cosme or
neighboring communities bring cut pieces to workshops or home workers who sew them together. These brokers then sell them at markets or
turn them over to manufacturers or retailers. The garment trade grew
rapidly in the early 1990s. By 1994, nearly one of every four households
had members who were involved in small-scale clothing manufacturing
as owners and/or workers. Nineteen percent of the households had one

or more merchants, many of whom were selling items produced in small workshops. In 2001 the proportion of households involved in garment production reached almost 30 percent (27.8), and 13 percent more were merchants who may also have been involved in garment manufacturing as producers, contractors, or vendors.[1]

The first workshops, which I think of as being independent, produced mainly for regional markets. The workshop owners designed (usually based on garments they saw in markets or magazines), made the patterns (often by taking apart a garment they purchased for copying), sewed, and marketed their products, primarily girls' dresses and women's skirts, themselves. In time these same producers began selling to large Mexican retailers at regional markets or to buyers who came directly to San Cosme.

Increasingly, many San Cosmeros/as also began following the procedure used in the large multinational assembly plants to produce what they call *maquila*. They sew precut pieces, especially polo shirts without collars and sweatpants that are brought to them by local or outside brokers who may work for large firms, usually retailers, or who sell the items themselves at markets. Today, the two types of workshop, *maquila* and independent, coexist sometimes within the same household. Another more recent development is that some of the larger workshops in San Cosme now rely on providing the cut pieces to be assembled by local *maquila* workshops to supplement the production of their own workers when demand is up or to replace their own workers whom they let go when demand is low. Some independent garment workshop owners have completely eliminated their own production. In one workshop that a few years ago employed about twenty workers, the two owners (a husband and wife) take a purchased garment, usually a woman's skirt, to a pattern maker. Then they have the garment cut by their own cutters. They no longer own any sewing machines, so the garments are assembled in other workshops. The couple then sell the completed garments at two large weekly regional markets in San Martín Texmelucan and Tepeaca. Another independent workshop owner said that his daughter-in-law makes the patterns and that they have a cutter, but they no longer do any sewing. In this way, he suggested, they do not have to deal with the *detalles* (details) of the workers.

Research on garment and other small-scale manufacturing elsewhere often suggests that workshops such as those in San Cosme operate with or without a craft-based flexibility. San Cosme's independent production corresponds to some extent to the craft-based flexibility described by

Figure 4.1. Large independent garment workshop, 1994

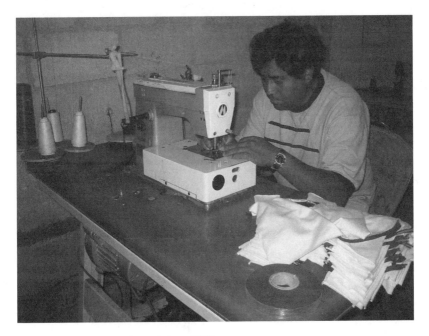

Figure 4.2. Small *maquila* workshop, 2005

Piore and Sabel (1984) and that relies on multiskilling and autonomy, whereas *maquila* production fits what Hsiung calls "non-craft-based flexibility" (1996, 32). As Hsiung points out, in craft-based flexibility, skilled workers use technological innovation to respond more flexibly to fluctuating demand. In non-craft-based flexibility, a competitive edge in a fluctuating market is achieved by relying on the increased productivity of workers, especially married women "who endure their multiple responsibilities at work and in the home 'flexibly'" (Hsiung 1996, 32). Their flexibility is based on juggling their different responsibilities and working longer hours on production for sale and fewer hours on their domestic or reproductive tasks when demand for their products is up. I would stress that the two kinds of flexibility may represent a continuum rather than two discrete types, with the labor of women and children being less autonomous and their flexibility consisting in whether and how much they produce. The need for flexibility is closely related to the volatile nature of the apparel market. Most of San Cosme's garment production is for the national market. But to understand its development, dilemmas, and prospects for further growth or failure, one needs to view it in the context of the international garment industry and the global flow of capital, technology, commodities, ideas, and images.

A Brief History of Garment Production

Although the Industrial Revolution was based in large part on the textile industry, since clothing was sewn at home or by tailors, the garment manufacturing industry did not emerge until relatively recently. In the one hundred and fifty years since its emergence, however, the textile/apparel industry, which was the first to become global, has become the most global of all industries. Almost since its beginnings, the apparel industry has been characterized by two different patterns: low-technology production in small-scale workshops and high-technology mass production. To some extent these patterns correspond to the distinction between fashion garments and standardized garments; that is, between designer clothing and staple or basic garments like T-shirts or underwear. But the two patterns are often connected, as larger firms subcontract some of their production to smaller firms.[2]

Because technological change in the garment industry has not been very extensive, especially in the sewing operations, start-up costs are relatively low. Even large garment firms have always tended to be smaller than those in other industries. Although multinational corporations in the textile and clothing industry do exist, even the largest are not as large, for example, as automobile firms. As Elson (1994) points out, the role of the developed countries in the industrial development of developing countries is different in the textile and clothing industry than in others. Whereas direct foreign investment in developing countries is significant in other industries, in the apparel industry there tends to be less direct foreign investment and more networks of licensees and subcontractors. Many of these are citizens of the developing countries. Furthermore, she notes, many of these firms in developing countries have internationalized to include those in still less developed countries (Elson 1994, 196). The networks between companies that characterize much of the apparel industry make tracing the involvement by different national parties and firms in the chain of production and distribution difficult,[3] but there is growing evidence suggesting important and discernible trends in the apparel industry globally and in Mexico.

Garments and Production on the Move

Beginning with Mexico's accession to the General Agreement on Tariffs and Trade (GATT) in 1986 and then the passage of NAFTA in 1994, internal tariffs between the United States, Canada, and Mexico were eliminated.[4] Many of the changes were to be phased out over a period of years, but others occurred immediately. Included among the first effects of NAFTA affecting garment production during the 1990s and at the turn of the twenty-first century that have impacted the Mexican garment industry are the following: a reduction of tariffs on textiles imported into Mexico; an increase in garments sold in Mexico made in the United States, made by U.S. firms in Mexico, or made of U.S. materials elsewhere; and an increase in garment exports from Mexico to the United States. We have already seen the impact of textile imports in putting much of the national Mexican textile industry out of business. In this section we examine the effects of trade liberalization on the apparel industry.

The increase of Mexican imports to the United States, especially of apparel, was so great that *Forbes* described it as a "massive shift by U.S. clothing manufacturers" from China (which had been the major exporter to the United States) to Mexico (Palmeri & Aguayo 1997).[5] The declining U.S. economy and the relocation of some U.S. producers to China in the last few years has reduced apparel imports from Mexico and increased those from China. Mexico remains a major source of U.S. apparel imports, but it was displaced by China by 2004 (U.S. Office of Textiles and Apparel, 2005).

Increased garment production for the U.S. market has contributed to the huge growth in employment in the *maquiladora* apparel sector from 25,300 in 1986 (when Mexico acceded to the General Agreement on Tariffs and Trade) to 270,000 in 2000.[6] But increased export production has also meant heightened sensitivity to the U.S. economy as well as to competition from elsewhere, especially China.

Trade liberalization (including changes before the actual passage of NAFTA) has not only increased Mexican exports to the United States it has also significantly affected U.S. exports to Mexico. During the 1980s, apparel imports increased more than twice as much as exports. Between 1980 and 1990, textile and garment exports from Mexico to the United States increased by 214 percent, but imports into Mexico increased by 500 percent (Suárez Aguilar 1994, 63). Because Mexico until recently limited imports from Asia, many of these imports were from Asia, especially China, via the United States (Darling, cited by Chinchilla & Hamilton 1994). The increased competition from imported garments contributed to a decline in Mexico's garment industry.

To deal with this increased competition, Mexican national apparel producers adopted several strategies. Although national producers have not been successful in penetrating export markets, some have become *maquiladoras* for U.S. firms (Hanson 1994). Others have begun to subcontract in Asia or have become importers.

A related strategy by national producers who have remained in garment production, either for the national market or as *maquiladoras,* has been to relocate to lower wage areas in Mexico. Until recently, garment production in Mexico was heavily dependent on small workshops concentrated in the Federal District. But by 1988 the share of Mexico's garment employment in Mexico City had declined from 55 percent to 29 percent (Hanson 1994, 234). In a process that Escobar Latapi and Martinez Castellanos (1991) call peripheralization, microenterprises move from larger cities, such as Guadalajara or the Federal District, to smaller cities and towns to find lower-wage workers.[7] In 1988, wages in the state of Tlaxcala were 56 percent of wages in the Federal District (Hanson, 1994).[8] That many of Tlaxcala's textile factory workers had lost their jobs or feared losing them made Tlaxcala even more attractive for such relocation.

As indicated in Chapter 2, *maquiladora* production was located initially at the U.S. border—El Paso/Ciudad Juárez, San Diego/Tijuana and Brownsville/Matamoros. A dispersal of *maquiladoras,* similar to the relocation of the national garment industry, has also occurred. According to one company that helps set up offshore production for international companies in Mexico, inland manufacturing is better for these companies because there is less competition for workers. Although its Web site does not mention the lower pay in the interior,[9] the company does point out that the inland workforce is more stable, has lower turnover, and that "the labor force is not saturated resulting in less competition for jobs (border *maquilas* may have to provide hot meals, taxi service, etc. to keep workers)" (http://offshore group.com.html/manu_inland.html).

The appeal of low wages, Tlaxcala's long history in the textile industry, the national textile industry's decline in the 1980s, the state's support of international investment through the construction of industrial corridors, tax exemptions, and infrastructure construction, and its convenient location and excellent roads attracted both the large and small sectors of the garment industry and national as well as international capital. During the 1990s, the garment sector became the state's most dynamic export sector (Alonso, 2000, 10). Of the 309 firms of all types listed by Tlaxcala's secretary of development (SEDECO) in 2001, seventy-one (23 percent) were garment firms (calculated from SEDECO) and at least 28 percent of the industrial workforce was in the apparel sector.[10] Although only eleven of the state's forty-eight foreign-owned firms are garment firms, as Kessler (1999, 583) points out, Tlaxcala has become one of the new production sites for California firms sourcing in Mexico. In addition, many of the national firms are manufacturing for U.S. firms, such as the Tarrant Apparel Group, a leading provider of private label casual apparel.

Cheap labor only partly explains the increasing shift from California to central Mexico. The availability of experienced male factory labor and of women with sewing skills, the clustering of garment production that provides necessary inputs such as fabric, which is available in the Federal District a few hours away and increasingly also locally, and the presence of contractors all contribute to relocation in Mexico, especially to Tlaxcala and the nearby state of Puebla, which has also become an important site of garment and textile production (Kessler 1999).

The growth of foreign-owned firms and firms producing for foreign firms for export, including *submaquilas* in which a *maquila* produces for another *maquila,* has become a major source of garment employment in Tlaxcala. In the neighboring community of Papalotla, for example, Azteca International, a U.S.-owned jeans producer involved in export to the United States, employed 2,700 people in 2001. For San Cosmeros/as, however, it is the small-scale, informal garment industry producing largely for the national market that has become the major source of employment.

Although some San Cosmeros/as work for multinational corporations or for *maquiladoras* or *submaquilas* producing for international firms, the major impact of such firms on San Cosme has been their effect on the informal, or nonregistered, garment sector. As competition from foreign firms forced Mexican national garment producers to look for other activities, many gave up producing for the national market. At the same time, as the income of working class Mexicans deteriorated, an opening was created for low-cost garment production in San Cosme. In 2001, a San Cosme independent producer might sell a skirt for twenty-five pesos to a vendor who sells it to the public for fifty pesos.[11] This growth of small-scale production in San Cosme fits with the overall trend in Mexican garment production. A study of formal-sector firms in the Mexican garment industry between 1982 and 1990 found that apparel industry growth has occurred at the extremes—with large (over one hundred people) and small companies (fifteen and fewer) (Suárez Aguilar 1994). During the eight-year period of that study, firms employing sixteen to one hundred people increased only 27 percent compared with 45 percent for microenterprises and 43 and 58 percent for medium (101 to 250 employees) and large firms (over 250).

San Cosme's small-scale garment producers stepped into the vacuum created by the slower relative growth in midsized firms. San Cosme had the comparative advantage of low wages as well as a long history in textile production and home sewing. Not only is the minimum wage in San Cosme lower than the Federal District but because San Cosme's *talleres* are informal, most of San Cosme's entrepreneurs avoid the costs associated with the formal sector, including benefits, overtime, and permanent employment.[12] Furthermore, garment workshop owners and workers subsidize production in a variety of ways. For example, many of the workers are at least partially supported by their families' agricultural production and/or the income-generating activities of other household members. Owners take advantage of family land or community electricity, and they too are often supported by their families' agricultural activities and/or the income generated by other members of their households. Consequently, San Cosmeros/as produce very cheaply and provide very inexpensive clothes.

Flexible Production

There has been a great deal of discussion in the literature on contemporary capitalism about flexible production and what some refer to as "the world after Fordism" (Dicken 1998, 165).[13] As Dicken points out, industrialization has gone through a long process characterized by "increasing efforts to mechanize and to control more closely the nature and speed of work" (1998, 165). The earliest workshops collected labor and divided it into specific tasks. Then the use of machinery was applied. In the early twentieth century, scientific management, or Taylorism, further divided labor to increase control and supervision. Then, also in the early twentieth century, Fordism led to the development of assembly lines to control pace in units that produced large volumes of standardized products for mass consumption (Dicken 1998, 165).

For Harvey, among others, the crisis in the postwar boom came in part because of the rigidity of such mass production systems. Mass production (and the capital that enabled it) was particularly rigid in that it produced large numbers of the same product. In addition, during the era of mass production, unions in the United States and other core countries experienced gains that critics equate with rigidity. Union success is also seen by such critics as responsible for big government, which may provide such benefits as social security, health care, and so forth. To deal with these rigidities (of big capital, big labor, and big government), a series of "novel experiments in the realms of industrial organization . . . have begun to take shape" (Harvey 1989, 145). These experiments may be the beginning of a new regime of accumulation characterized by flexibility with regard to labor processes, labor markets, products, and patterns of consumption (Harvey 1989, 147).

Although there are important differences among them, most analysts focus on the idea that commitment to products and/or workers is flexible. Products produced change rapidly and no commitment is made to labor about wages, benefits, specific tasks to be performed, or length of employment. As Stinchcombe suggests, the critical criterion is "short production runs of many different products . . . produced nearly as cheaply as long runs of standardized goods" (1987, 186). The cheaper cost of flexible production has led many observers to suggest that it is necessarily associated with sweating and exploited labor.[14] Piore and Sabel, who have one of the most optimistic views of flexible special- ization, argue that sweating is not inherent in it. For them, "Flexible specialization is a strategy of permanent innovation: accommodation to ceaseless change, rather than an effort to control it" (1984, 17). Sweat- ing is a feature only of flexible specialists who fail to innovate (1984, 263). They suggest also that competition, thus exploitation, can be con- trolled by the "creation, through politics, of an industrial community that restricts the forms of competition to those favoring innovation" (1984, 17). Their optimistic view is not shared by all; others, especially those who see flexible production or specialization as growing with glo- balization and inequality, are less sanguine.[15]

Garment production in San Cosme is characterized by flexibility in la- bor, markets, and products. Underlying it is a great deal of innovation. In the next section I discuss flexibility in garment production in San Cosme and the constant effort on the part of the producers to innovate. In the following chapter I show that despite the many innovations that San Cos- meros/as have made, innovation and sweating do go hand in hand here.

Ceaseless Change and Innovation

Since the first workshop was begun there in the late 1980s, I have been back to San Cosme on seven different visits ranging from two days in the summer of 1993, when I saw a workshop for the first time, to a field stay of five days a week for four months in the fall of 2001 and short visits of a few days in the summer of 2004 and two weeks in the sum- mer of 2005. Not only has the number of people involved in garment production grown, but there are no garment producers who have not changed what they produce, how much they produce, for whom they produce, or whether they produce. There has been constant change.

This contrasts starkly to the continuities that persisted in San Cosme despite important changes in the 1970s and 1980s. Although over those two decades the number of factory workers increased and the number of *campesinos/as* declined, most of the factory workers continued to work in the same factories. Even if an individual worker moved, for example, from a factory in the Federal District to a factory in Puebla, both were likely to be textile factories where other San Cosmeros were also work- ing. Some people began working in other kinds of factories, especially

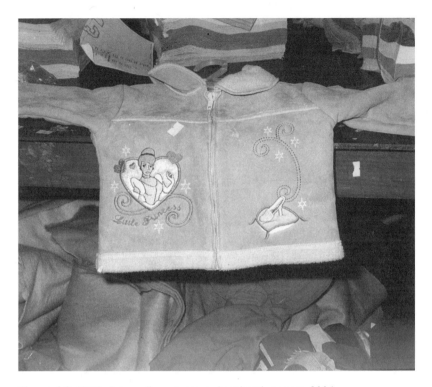

Figure 4.3. "Little Princess" computer-embroidered garment, 2004

for multinationals, such as Volkswagen or a nearby Monsanto chemical plant, but they too were likely to continue in the same factory until the 1980s when gradually they, like everybody else, began losing their jobs.

Garment production has varied more widely over a relatively short period of time. People who were not garment producers become garment producers. People who were garment producers give it up; some take up garment production, give it up and then take it up again. Independent producers become *maquila* producers, and *maquila* producers become independent producers; some try doing both at the same time. Some people who had their own workshops become workers for others. Some have supplemented or replaced garment production with fabric making. Others have begun to specialize in computer-aided embroidery on garments that others produce. There has been an overall pattern in the community of increased involvement in garment production (and concerns about consequent increases in competition), but it is difficult to discern many continuous trends other than increasing participation, growth of *maquila* production compared with independent production, and increasing withdrawal from garment production by some producers and a slowing of growth after the initial explosive expansion in the early 1990s.

Two Independent *Talleres*

In the late 1980s, fearing he would lose his job operating a weaving machine in a textile factory in Mexico City, Don Alberto (now in his late thirties) asked a friend to teach him to sew. He taught his wife, Doña María, who had secretarial but not sewing skills, and they began making girls' dresses on two machines they bought at the time. They would buy a dress in a market, take the dress apart, make a pattern, and proceed to make their own dresses. He went to Mexico City weekly to buy fabric, and together they sold the dresses at the large weekly markets on Fridays in Tepeaca and on Tuesdays in San Martín. His brothers and one of her sisters also began garment production. Another sister worked for a while as a contractor and more recently as a *taller* worker. Sometimes family members help each other selling, with labor, or with supplies. Today, Don Alberto and Doña María are among the most successful garment producers. During the busy periods they often have as many as forty workers. They sell directly to retail stores, many of which are regular customers at the markets or send buyers weekly to San Cosme to pick up their garments. Other customers are vendors who sell the garments at other markets. One of his brothers, who was also a large producer, having now invested in weaving equipment so that he can make fabric, has switched to fabric production. The couple changed to women's skirts for a period but then switched back to girls' dresses. Their teenaged sons are studying in high school and university; occasionally they help out in the workshop.

Also in the late 1980s, Don Jaime, a man about forty years old, also feared he would lose his factory job. He had taken a tailoring course some time before. He suggested to his sister (who had learned to sew in high school) and her husband, who had recently lost his job and was buying and selling clothes from regional suppliers and at regional markets, that they begin sewing at the sister's house on their mother's pedal sewing machine and on a second one that the sister had gotten as a

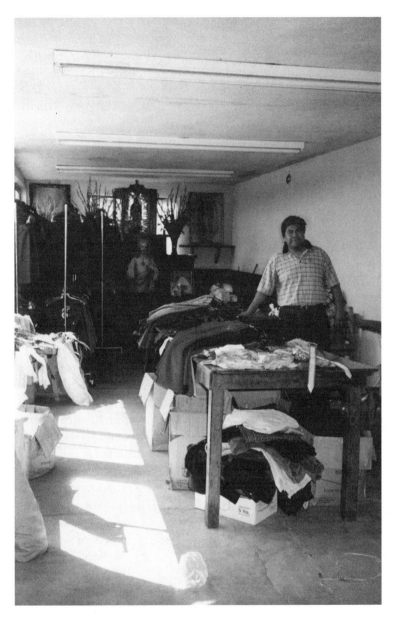

Figure 4.4. Medium independent workshop, 2001

wedding gift. They began making skirts and selling them at some of the smaller markets. Eventually, he set up a separate workshop in his own house. In the mid-1990s, the sister and her husband were among the most successful producers. By the late 1990s, however, they had closed their business because of financial problems. The market had declined and their garments were not selling well. Don Jaime and Doña Ema, his wife, who runs the workshop when he is away or when they need more labor, now make polo shirts in a midsized workshop that is moderately successful. They have twelve machines: three *overs* (overlock machines), five *rectas* (for straight stitching), one *collarete* (for collars), one *ojalera* (for buttonholes), and a *bastilladora* (for doubling the hem). Usually they employ five workers in addition to Don Jaime. Often they make small batches, fewer than a hundred pieces, of a design in accordance with a client's specifications. More often they make what they think they can sell. Don Jaime designs the shirts and sells them in the weekly markets in San Martín on Tuesdays and three hours away in Teziutlán on Fridays. When necessary, Doña Ema and their teenaged son, a university student, also sew.

Three *Maquila* Workshops

At about the same time, in the late 1980s, others began sewing *maquila*. Contractors, first from elsewhere and then from San Cosme, began giving out piecework. One woman, for example, sewed large sacks for a fellow San Cosmero. He got the sacks from a company that produced the pieces and he distributed them to San Cosmeras. Eventually, his supplier went elsewhere for workers. Many San Cosmeros/as now sew collarless T-shirts for contractors from Puebla or Zacatelco, a community about ten miles away. Today, many individuals and small workshops do *maquila*. One contractor from Puebla has bought a house in the community in which he sometimes stays and from which he works distributing and collecting men's pants and Bermuda shorts, usually to individual women who have the two machines necessary. As more people in the community now have machines (usually one *over* and one *recta)* on which to do *maquila,* the independent workshops now also use home workers or *maquila* shops. When demand is great, Don Jaime uses three *maquila* workshops in addition to the five workers in his workshop. Some workshops let almost all their workers go during the slow periods and rely on *maquila* until demand increases.

In the mid-1990s, Don Pedro and Doña Julia (now in their late forties) began doing collarless T-shirts for a contractor from a neighboring community. Eventually they developed their own business producing T-shirts that two of their sons market in Oaxaca. In addition to their own workshop where they now also make their own fabric, they rely on *maquila*. Doña Petra (forty-one years old) began doing *maquila* in the winter of 2001. Her husband, who has another job, is very rarely involved in the business. She does piecework frequently for Don Pedro and Doña Julia (whose daughter is married to Doña Petra's son) and for about four other contractors. She has five machines: two collar machines, one *recta* and two *overs*. She usually has five workers in addition to herself, and when she is rushed her teenaged daughter and brothers help.

Doña Luisa (age forty-three) and Don Jorge (thirty-seven) have three embroidery machines on which they have been working for others (including Don Jaime). She has been doing the work for three years and he, a former *obrero*, began two years ago. Although they embroider the word *Nike* on some of the shirts, neither they nor the contractors are producing for Nike. Their teenaged daughter, a student, occasionally helps them.

When Doña Esperanza (twenty-seven) married Don Marcos (also twenty-seven) seven years ago, the man for whom she had been working (who did *maquila* for a contractor from elsewhere) offered to loan them an *over* and a *recta* on which they could sew T-shirts for him. After a few years, he said he needed money and they bought the used machines from him. They continued to *maquila* for others. Then they bought another *over*, a *recta*, and a collar machine, and in addition to doing *maquila* they also began producing their own designs (T-shirts and T-shirt dresses) and selling them in San Martín. They had one fifteen-year-old girl working for them. In the fall of 2001 they were finding business very slow. They let the one worker go and started selling sandwiches on Sundays at the town plaza. They were hoping that the garment business would pick up.

Ceaseless change is apparent in what is produced and by whom in all these cases. San Cosme's producers change from T-shirts to skirts to pants and from children's to adults' garments. Few have not produced more than one type of garment. They have also innovated technologically by buying additional machines, including those for collars, buttons, buttonholes, printing, embroidery, and fabric. Even when they are making the same type of garments, there is constant change in fabric and style. When I visited in 2001, the owner of one workshop, for example, which makes mostly children's clothes including shirts and pants, had just purchased a pair of cargo shorts made in Vietnam that she was in the process of copying. The owners of another workshop said they never used the same fabric for more than a week, even if they were producing for the same retailer or vendor. Changes are made in response to changing availability and prices of supplies and demand for new styles.

Change also characterizes how much is produced and for which market. Workshops may employ thirty people ten hours a day, seven days a week when they are busy before Christmas, for example, and are producing for large retailers or just a few people a few hours a day when they are producing only for a local street market. A woman who does *maquila* may do a hundred pieces herself in a week or, if pushed to get things done quickly, may rely on others as well. In one case, a woman had her son (a government worker), her husband (a retired factory worker), a teenager who lived with the family and did domestic work, and the visiting anthropologist all assisting her when she needed to have a hundred pieces completed in a few days.

For whom San Cosmeros/as work also changes. Most of San Cosme's production has been for the national informal market, but some producers work for the formal market, particularly retailers in Guadalajara or Chiapas. At least one *maquila* workshop, which is now out of business, used to produce for export to the United States, and several owners report that they are now working for contractors who distribute in Guatemala and other Latin American markets. Most say they are willing to produce for export if it pays as well as the national market, but they have not been approached. Some owners suggested that the level of quality control demanded by exporters is too great for them.

Owners and workers are also flexible with regard to skill. Most workers can operate at least two machines: the *over* and the *recta*. Some owners, such as Don Jaime, expect workers to be, in his words, "multifunctional" and able to operate any of the six different kinds of machines in his *taller*. Owners and workers have also developed the skills to design as well as make their products and to predict what the market will want and where.

Despite all their flexibility, many workshops have closed. Production demands a great investment of time, effort, and resources, and the returns at any given point may be very small if the market is down. Everyone in San Cosme today is aware of the employment that garment production has generated. People often say that an important and positive change in the community is that work is now available in San Cosme. In the early 1990s there was a great deal of optimism about the garment industry. It had grown from no workshops in the late 1980s to hundreds in 1994. People pointed to the success of many of the workshops and noted that this owner or that owner had "a car of the year" and a new large house. It seemed also that many families were encouraging their children to go into the garment business rather than continuing their studies and pursuing professional careers.[16]

By 2001, the garment industry seemed to have lost some of its appeal. In the new millennium, there is more concern about competition from China (which was just being admitted to the World Trade Organization) as well as about their neighbors in San Cosme. People complained about the adverse effects of sewing on their eyes and backs, and everyone knew that workshops came and went. School attendance for young people has increased, and while paid work, especially in garment workshops, is still a popular choice for young women and young men, it is not growing as rapidly as it did in the early 1990s. When asked what they hoped their sons or daughters would do, several workshop owners said they wanted them to do something else. Young workers are, for the most part, still fairly optimistic about garment work despite concerns with low wages and frequent slow periods. But few young workers anticipate doing what they are doing forever. Most of the women envision getting married. Many of the young male and female workers express the hope that through education they will be able to go into another kind of work. Some, but fewer than in the past, express the hope that some day they will have their own *taller*.

Why has flexible garment production lost some of its allure? As Nancy Green points out, flexibility can exist at two levels: "the global level of an economic sector and the firm level of work organization" (1997, 6). Most analyses of flexibility, she suggests, have stressed the global level. But, Green argues, the two levels cannot be separated, and we must ask, flexibility for whom? In the next chapter I discuss the gains and pains of flexibility in the garment industry and suggest that the benefits vary according to whether one looks at the global or at the work level. Flexible production has enormous advantages for retailers, manufacturers, and retailer/manufacturers who face intense competition for consumers. For workers, owners, and worker-owners of small flexible firms, however, the possibilities for gain are more illusory. Furthermore, those possibilities vary by gender and wealth. As the next chapter discusses, different segments of the community have benefited more than others. These segments also differ in their ability to withstand further difficulties and in their prospects for alternative activities and futures.

CHAPTER 5

Making It in the Garment Industry

Doña Gloria, a vivacious and attractive woman who was in her early forties in 2001, is one of the more successful *taller* owners. In the late 1970s, she was one of the small but growing number of employed young women in the community. She worked for a few years as a hairdresser in Puebla before she married. Then she stopped working for pay and had a child. Shortly thereafter, she and her husband separated. She went back to paid work in the early 1980s, this time as a factory worker in a *maquiladora* in Tlaxcala where women's undergarments were made to be sold in the United States. When a new ceramic tile factory opened in San Cosme in the mid-1980s, she was among their first workers. In 1989, having worked there for four years, she was earning the relatively good salary of 125,000 pesos ($50) a week. Although this was more than *taller* workers who were earning weekly between 60,000 and 85,000 pesos, or teachers and nurses earning about 100,000 pesos, and only slightly less than male factory workers who had been working for some time and earning 140,000 pesos, she was thinking of leaving that job. She disliked the ceramic dust powder that was ever present (and necessitated bathing and changing clothes every day before leaving work) and thought she could earn more as a merchant.

The oldest of her three brothers had recently bought a truck and was thinking about quitting his factory job to sell clothes to consumers or other vendors at regional markets. She decided to go into business with him. By 1994, each of her three brothers had a clothing workshop with about eight machines apiece. Doña Gloria continued selling (mostly the garments her oldest brother produced) because she felt that she did not have enough family labor to open her own workshop.[1] By 1997, however, she had remarried. She had a new child and a year-old *taller* with six machines and thirteen workers, including four cutters, a person to hang up the garments, and an all-around helper. In 2001, after only five years in operation, she had added two floors of workspace to her house (on land she inherited from her parents) and was making and selling as much as eight thousand garments a week. Her oldest daughter recently was married, and four hundred guests were present at the celebration. Her younger child attends a private primary school in a neighboring community that, in addition to the usual subjects, offers English and swimming lessons.

Doña Gloria's story is not unique. About twenty families in San Cosme have become quite successful in the garment business, and they all have what Doña Gloria and her brothers needed to succeed. This chapter describes and analyzes the factors that contribute to such success. It shows also that the majority of people in the garment business are not owners but workers and that most are owners of small *maquila* workshops. As we will see, garment production does not require a great deal of capital, though some is needed. Where and how people get access to capital is linked to other factors, especially family wealth, gender, and age. The necessary labor and skills are not that hard to come by in San Cosme, but different segments of the community are in better or worse positions to acquire labor and skills. Men from families with more land and other resources are in a more advantaged position and thus more likely to be owners of workshops. Women, especially those from poorer families and those with few kin in the community, have either very small workshops or they work at home or in the workshops of others.

Some might argue that the fact that these poorer women, despite their relatively disadvantaged positions, now have employment means that their situations have improved compared with the past when few jobs were available for women, other than even lower-paying domestic employment or agricultural labor.[2] Others, however, point out that their wages are low, their jobs insecure, and work conditions, which critics liken to sweatshops, are often very poor. Critics also point to the precarious position even of those who appear to be successful. While a discussion of the garment industry in San Cosme alone cannot decide whether the benefits of workshop work outweigh the disadvantages, it can reveal some of the ways in which new and existing inequalities are created, maintained, and/or changed. Since much of today's global apparel industry is based on similar small-scale production, some of the lessons learned from San Cosme may be applicable elsewhere.[3]

Making it in the garment industry depends on local, national, and global patterns of production and distribution. Although patterns at these three levels ultimately need to be viewed together, different ones predominate at each level. Consequently, we must examine them separately. The first part of this chapter describes the prerequisites for garment production that derive primarily from local patterns: access to capital; a kin network and kin labor; and commercial, designing, and sewing skills. The second part focuses on gender and class and the influence of national patterns of occupational segregation. The third part of the chapter looks at San Cosme's garment industry in relation to the larger world of global production and distribution of which it is a part. Here I bring together local, national, and global patterns to suggest that San Cosmeros/as, whether workers or successful owners, may not in the long run survive in the garment industry. If we look at the history of garment production and at the competition in the world today, San Cosme's workshops appear to be only a temporary phase. I suggest in subsequent chapters, however, that garment production has made a more permanent mark. It may not persist, but its consequences, I think, will.

The Wealth of Kinship: Kin Contacts and Material Resources

As indicated in Chapter 4, garment workshops have been started by San Cosmeros/as with a minimum of expense for machinery or training. Some people, usually women, had sewing skills, but even if they did not, most could usually learn to sew from a relative, friend, or neighbor. Machines were often purchased with the severance pay that downsized factory workers received. Some people began using noncommercial machines (like the brother and sister who used machines received as wedding gifts years before). Many of the early independent producers, like Doña Gloria and her brothers, began buying and selling apparel and then used their earnings from that trade to purchase commercial sewing machines and begin their own production. Now that garments have been produced in the community for some time, used machines are available, often from owners giving up garment production. At the same time, however, the start-up costs, especially for independent production, have increased. The number of different machines used has grown, and with that the costs of machines have risen as producers make more complex garments with buttons, buttonholes, collars, and other details. The minimum requirement in an independent workshop

Figure 5.1. Wedding present (two sewing machines), 2001

is now three different types of machines: an *over*, a *recta*, and a collar machine. Even some *maquila* work now requires more than just the two basic types that sufficed in the past. Although previously owned *overs* and *rectas* are available locally, other types of machines still have to be purchased new. Furthermore, sewing skills and sewing machines are not all that is needed for garment production. In addition to capital for the machines and sewing skills, access to labor, space, and commercial and other skills are all necessary. Additionally, when the volatile garment market is down, access to an alternative source of economic support is critical. Kin in San Cosme provide access to the material, social, and human capital necessary for garment production.

Lash and Urry, among others, have noted the importance of what they refer to as *"économies de famille"* (1994, 179) for entrepreneurial success among immigrant families. Few studies, however, have explored how and why such families are the basis for entrepreneurial activities in some contexts but not others or which families and/or households are more likely to succeed in those contexts. Examining the flexible kinship system in San Cosme sheds some light on these questions.

San Cosme has a bilateral kinship system in which descent is reckoned through both males and females. Inheritance is also bilateral, with males and females inheriting equally. In addition to the bilateral kinship system and to relations established through marriage, *compadrazgo* (ritual kinship) further extends kinship relations. *Compadrazgo* in San Cosme, as elsewhere in Mexico, stresses ties formed by godparenthood between the co-parents (the godchild's parents and godparents) and often establishes long-term relations between them. Although godparents may serve in more than one capacity, godparents of confirmation, for example, are also usually godparents of marriage. But San Cosmeros/as do not usually have consanguineal or affinial kin as *compadres* and people related by *compadrazgo* are not supposed to marry. Thus, the *compadrazgo* system widens one's kin network.

What distinguishes San Cosme's system is the importance of kinship, including ritual kinship, and the system's flexibility. This pattern goes back at least to the family economy and has persisted despite the proletarianization of the 1960s and early 1970s. As I discuss in Chapter 6, although there are indications that with increasing economic differentiation, kinship connections may be narrowing so that the circle of kin to whom one is obligated is smaller among the more prosperous, the importance of kinship for most San Cosmeros/as continues to be stressed in ideology and practice. What this means is that families, usually nuclear or extended, are embedded in larger webs of kin relations. People expect to exchange labor, food, and other resources, and they do so frequently.

This system of bilateral kinship, marriage, and *compadrazgo* surrounds individuals with a large network of people on whom they can draw in a variety of contexts. The system is broad enough so that individuals know many of their kin (through meeting them at life cycle events and the annual saint's day celebration throughout their lives as well as in everyday activities), but they do not have many formal obligations to kin beyond their immediate families to constrain them. People are supposed to invite kin related to them by males and females through their parents' first cousins to weddings, baptisms, and funerals, and closer kin, such as siblings, are expected to assist in the preparations. Beyond these requirements, however, people can relate to their kin in a variety of ways. Some kin, for example, regularly exchange agricultural labor. Some hire other kin to work along with non-kin in their fields. Furthermore, the nature of the relationships can and does change. As a family's children grow, they may rely more on the labor of their immediate family or, as their children spend more time in school, they may rely less on the labor of their immediate family and more on other kin either for pay or in exchange for their labor.

The system's flexibility has enabled it to change and still remain important. Yanagisako (2002) has noted that often when analysts discuss kinship and family firms in Asia, for example, they essentialize family relations and treat them as unchanging or they deal with such families as resources to be drawn upon in a utilitarian fashion. She proposes that kinship is neither an unchanging basis of certain capitalisms (such as Italian or Asian) nor a simple adaptation to capitalism. Like the family firms Yanagisako studied in Italy, the flexible system in San Cosme allows San Cosmeros/as to use kinship resources (including ideologies and sentiments involving cooperation, support, and assistance) while they are, in fact, modifying their kinship practices and ideas to fit particular historical circumstances. For example, San Cosmeros/as have more often reciprocally exchanged agricultural labor, especially with siblings, siblings-in-law, and cousins. As more men went to work in factories, men increasingly relied on kin to help them get factory jobs. The absence of proletarian men led to hiring kin and non-kin rather than exchanging agricultural labor.

Although kinship is important among all San Cosmeros/as, more affluent families have advantages through kinship as well as wealth. Families that are better off materially are more likely to have more diverse social contacts through kinship and to have more extensive social networks, which give them ties and resources that can be used in garment production. More affluent families can afford to celebrate life cycle and ritual events and get together with kin more frequently. "Getting together assures that people know who their kin are, where they live, and what they can do" (Rothstein 1999, 584). Not only are better-off families likely to know more kin and to know more about their kin because their celebrations are more frequent, their kin and non-kin networks are more diverse. This diversity may provide access to different goods and services. Most of the families who are better off today are those whose members included factory workers in the past. As indicated in Chapter 3, their factory employment in Mexico City or Puebla increased the likelihood of their marrying someone who is not local or of having ritual kin from elsewhere. This increased the diversity of their kin and what kin can give to each other. In one case, for example, one of the first women to become a *taller* owner learned to sew while she was studying in secondary school in Mexico City. At that time there was still no secondary school in San Cosme. Through her father's factory work, her family had the contacts and resources that allowed her to continue her schooling outside the community.

Kin networks are directly and indirectly involved in garment production in a variety of ways. All of the independent workshops are owned or run by a male-female pair of close kin, usually husband and wife, but there are also son-and-mother or brother-and-sister pairs. One partner, usually the male, handles the external contacts and the other, usually the female, handles the internal management. Individuals who are not part of such a pair, such as Doña Gloria before she remarried, are unable to establish a workshop. In another case, a son tried to get his mother to agree to run a workshop. Although he had purchased machines and the mother sometimes did *maquila* for others, she did not want to supervise a workshop and successfully resisted. Eventually, he sold the machines.

The most successful workshops often began with several pairs of kin working together and learning from each other. One sibling may be the initial designer. As others pick up that and other skills and as the business grows, they may develop separate firms. Over time, kin often do separate their firms (as in Doña Gloria's case), but many continue to cooperate. They may lend each other labor, fabric, or other supplies; they may provide transportation for each other to markets or to purchase supplies; and sometimes they sell together or for each other.

Garment production always begins with kin labor. In some cases, all of the initiators are owners and benefit (or bear the costs) equally. In other cases, the benefits are not equally distributed. Men usually handle the financial aspects of buying materials, hiring labor, and selling the finished products. Women, usually wives, may be given part of the profit (often to run the household). I was surprised when discussing the possibility of visiting New York with one of the more successful entrepreneurial couples when the wife, an outspoken woman who plays a major role in the business, suggested that the husband could probably get a visa because he had a bank account and would thus be able to get the necessary papers, whereas she would have more trouble getting into the United States.

As *talleres* grow they rely more on paid labor, but smaller *talleres* and larger ones, in their earlier phases, rely very heavily on unpaid family labor. Even a home worker may need to pull in other family members when she is in a rush or requires a different skill.[4] For almost all garment producers, kin provide the reservoir of skills and at least some of the labor that is necessary. Independent production, which is the most lucrative, requires not only sewing skills but also designing, pattern making, grading, cutting, and commercial skills to obtain fabric and market the final product. *Maquila* production requires fewer different skills but also draws upon skills other than sewing. In one case, for example, a woman doing *maquila* was supposed to put together eleven hundred pieces to make one hundred pairs of children's sweatpants. She was given a few days to complete the garments but no instructions on how to fit the pieces together. Unfortunately, the pieces were cut wrong, and the parts of different-sized garments were all mixed together. It was not until her husband, who was helping, realized that one part needed to be recut that they figured out how the pieces fit together. Although she was responsible for the *maquila*, she was assisted by her husband (who sorted the pieces by size), a seventeen-year-old grandson who sewed, and his seventeen-year-old wife who folded the completed garments while she watched their young child. The woman responsible gave the younger couple a portion of her earnings. In another case, a woman doing *maquila* had trouble threading one of her sewing machines. She kept trying to follow the directions (which were not in Spanish). Later in the day, a young male cousin came to get help from her son about a personal matter. Since his family had a *taller*, he was able to show her how to thread the machine.

Access to kin with the variety of skills that are needed for independent or *maquila* production and the willingness to work in the garment industry are crucial requirements for success. In one case, for example, two sisters began *maquila* production together with two machines (an *over* and a *recta*). After a short time, one of the sisters decided she did not like sewing. The other sister has continued to do *maquila*. Although she is very fast and occasionally her husband, a mason, helps her, she has not been able to expand the business without the assistance of additional kin. Her parents are interested mainly in agricultural production, and she has no other siblings or children. Her husband's family lives elsewhere.

Another independent workshop was on the verge of failure. Competition (within San Cosme and with producers elsewhere) is increasing the need for more labor and greater investments in technology. The couple who owns the workshop had begun it as a *maquila* shop in 1998. By 2001 they had five machines of three types (a collar machine, two *overs*, and two *rectas*). They rely usually on their own labor and the labor of one paid worker. They make T-shirts, polo shirts with collars, and skirts or pants with elastic waists. Recently, this workshop began experiencing difficulties. As the market declined, they let their one paid worker go. But they could not produce cheaply enough to support even themselves.

Since many of their competitors now rely on subcontracting to kin or non-kin usually in San Cosme so that they can provide larger quantities and lower prices, this workshop may also be forced into subcontracting. They now sell only one day a week at one market. They would need more cash and more labor to produce more so that they could sell at a second location. They could increase production by subcontracting but they would need more cash. They cannot increase production with family labor. Her family lives elsewhere and his kin, although from San Cosme, have other employment. His family might help out, but they cannot provide much labor. Given limited labor and cash, there is a good chance they will have to go back to doing *maquila* for others.

The home-based nature of production in San Cosme facilitates the incorporation of kin, including those who are engaged in other work. It allows women, especially, to do garment work while also doing domestic activities. It enables those who have other employment to help in the evenings or on weekends. When a workshop grows, reliance on paid labor generally increases, and often some of those who were providing unpaid labor withdraw except during peak periods. Wives may withdraw from garment production to allow more time for domestic activities. Successful owners sometimes hire others to perform domestic tasks. In one case of *maquila* production, the husband reduced his involvement in garment production to attend the university. The wife and one or two paid workers did most of the sewing. He picked up the pieces that were to be sewn in Puebla, delivered the finished garments, and sewed when they were rushed or during school vacations. Despite their lack of involvement on a regular basis, these kin continue to provide labor, especially during busy times.

Kin who are part of one's immediate family (spouses, sons, daughters, and parents) are most likely to be pulled in for garment work when demand has increased, and those living nearby, either in the house or in adjacent houses, a common occurrence because of inheritance, are more likely to be relied upon. But kin elsewhere will often assist. The grandson and his wife in the example above did not live in the same household as the grandmother whom they helped. They usually visited every day, and if the grandmother needed help they often helped.

Garment workshops also depend on family space. All of them began in family space, often a bedroom. Because of this lack of spatial separation between work and home, social and productive activities frequently occur together. If a relative (including fictive kin) or close neighbor visits a family with a family workshop and the person he or she is visiting is working while they socialize, the visitor will often help out by folding, hanging up garments, picking off threads, or even sewing. The visitor may be given some cash, but it is a gift rather than a carefully calculated amount.[5] Even young children, living or visiting a garment-producing household, often help out by picking off threads, hanging up garments, or ironing, as in the case of one ten-year-old. The domestic location of garment production means also that paid domestic workers may be pulled into garment production when there is pressure to complete an order.

While the location of work in domestic spaces may enable some to generate income when they otherwise might not by, for example, combining child care and income generation, having a workshop in the home also usually means that the house is taken over by machines. Doña Martina and her husband, Don Teodoro, built a new house on land she inherited from her parents and furnished it with a living room set and a dining room set while they were clothes vendors. Then they set up their workshop. Although the machines were in a room off the living room, the red velvet couch in the living room was covered with garments, stacks of clothes were everywhere, and workers streamed through the whole house six and sometimes seven days a week from morning to night. Workshop owners often add a room or another floor to house their production when they are able to do so (and many never can). Until they do, workspace is family space, and it is impossible to separate work and daily life or to get away from garment production.

Another, often hidden form of kin assistance that is also facilitated by but does not require coresidence is the child care that frees garment producers to do business. Grandmothers often care for the children of women working in *talleres* (either their own or others'). Older siblings are called upon to care for their younger siblings while parents are working in or outside the home. Sons and daughters may also take over other domestic tasks that their parents do not have time for because of their workshop activities. In one case, a teenaged daughter cooked many of the meals while the parents produced and sold the garments. In another case of a *maquila* workshop in which both the husband and wife sewed, the wife usually took care of domestic tasks, and the husband, agricultural ones. The two children studied, but when the parents were rushed, the daughter helped with domestic tasks and the son took over the father's agricultural chores.

Kin networks thus serve as the source for a great deal of unpaid labor and of the various kinds of skilled labor on which the garment industry depends. They are also important in recruiting paid labor; the information exchanged via kin plays a major role in identifying who is available for employment and what skills they have. Both *maquila* and independent production require personnel skills to recruit and maintain one's labor force. Although periodically there are announcements over the loudspeaker system for *taller* workers, owners rely more on personal contacts to, as Hsiung (1996, 71) describes it, "discover" workers. Men and boys, even though less often employed in the workshops, often serve as the links through which labor is recruited. Especially as workshop labor has become scarcer, kinship ties and events are used as occasions to recruit labor. In one case, for example, a busy entrepreneur who did *maquila* for a contractor from another community kept pressing his cousin every time they met to *maquila* for him.

The kin relationship between workers and owners also helps employers maintain authority.[6] Workers in San Cosme rarely confront employers directly about work conditions. Once they have some experience, however, they frequently leave to work at another workshop. Given the multistranded ties of most people in San Cosme to many others, as well as a labor shortage, workers usually have ties to many potential employers. New workers and those who have few kin ties, usually because they have married into the community or have been hired from elsewhere, are at the greatest disadvantage in recruiting labor or finding other work in the garment industry. For them, kinship ties give the employers a distinct advantage.

Kin also provide information and cooperation for marketing products. Sometimes they help each other by sharing a post at a market or selling the other's garments. One of the more successful families markets their garments in Oaxaca with the help of the kin of a daughter-in-law from Oaxaca. One of the members of another family is a leader at a major market. His political position enhances the opportunities for all his kin.

Kin and Their Material Resources

It is important to stress that no one is San Cosme is wealthy and that even small differences in resources can be significant. Almost everyone in the community can get at least one sewing machine, either by borrowing the money or from family funds, to become a *maquila* producer. More recently, machines could be purchased in San Cosme or Puebla on the installment plan. Independent production, however, which is more lucrative, requires a greater investment of money as well as time. Better-off families are more likely to be able to buy sewing machines; to buy, rent, or convert more space for a workshop; to buy one or more vehicles to transport garments; to pay for a post in one of the busier and therefore more costly markets; to support a son or daughter in further schooling where they can learn sewing, designing, or other skills necessary in the business; or to support family members in the garment business when demand in that industry is down. Many people purchase their machines with their own money, often the severance pay or bonus from the husband's factory work. Others get funds to purchase machines as gifts or loans, usually from parents or siblings. Recently, it has become the practice for the parents of a bride to give the newlyweds commercial sewing machines (instead of furniture) as a wedding present. Some *taller* owners have developed their workshops by selling land they inherited. Better-off families can afford to buy or help some of their members buy machines (including the larger number of different machines that are now required), fabric, trucks or campers, and market posts. They can also provide the larger space necessary for all of the steps (designing, cutting, sewing, and storing) involved in independent production.

The material resources of kin are also crucial in subsidizing the garment industry. Kin underwrite garment production with multiple livelihoods. As indicated in Chapter 3, even when San Cosmeros/as relied on relatively well-paid jobs in textile factories, they combined industrial work with subsistence cultivation and sometimes other income-generating activities, such as running a store or mill. During the crisis of the 1980s, multiple livelihoods became even more common. Whereas some proletarian families had begun to cut down on their subsistence production prior to the crisis and rely almost exclusively on the wages of a single male breadwinner, by 1989 most households had more than one member generating an income, and they depended on the pooling of wages, cash, subsistence products, and unpaid labor. Today, that same pattern of multiple livelihoods supports the garment industry. In some cases, one spouse, usually the husband, continues in his/her formal sector employment and is involved in the workshop or in selling its products on weekends and in the evenings. In other cases, retired factory workers have pensions that help underwrite their garment production. Other households supplement income from garment production and/or trade by having a store, animals, and/or other sources of income. The households of most of the workshop owners and workers also at least raise some corn for their families and sometimes for sale.

Figure 5.2. Workshop owner in garden, 2005

Some supplemental support is regularly provided by kin, even if it is only the provision of space, corn, or electricity.[7] Because of the volatility of the garment market, kin also provide indispensable support that enables garment producers to survive the frequent downturns in the apparel market. In one case, for example, when an independent *taller* had to close down, the family helped their daughter migrate to the United States for employment. Eventually, with the help of the remittances she sent, they were able to go back into garment production.

Thus, garment production involves a network of kin who help garment producers in a variety of ways, sometimes with and for cash. Although everybody in San Cosme has kin, better-off families—until recently, families of men who worked for many years in textile factories—are more likely to have the material resources and kinship ties (based in part also on their greater material resources) to facilitate successful garment production. These more affluent families are able to set up and later expand production, finance marketing, and support those in the garment business when the unstable apparel market is down. These families have also been more able to maintain their kinship ties because they can afford to have the various life cycle celebrations for which kin get together and to attend kin events elsewhere. They usually also have a more diverse kin network on which to draw for more varied assistance. But it is not only wealth and kinship that afford different opportunities. One's gender and the larger Mexican occupational structure also influence one's likelihood of success in the garment industry.

Gender in and Beyond San Cosme

In the family economy that prevailed in San Cosme until recently, relations between women and men were relatively egalitarian. Both played important roles in agricultural production, and domestic tasks were the responsibility of both as well. Women and men were subordinate in the public sphere to more powerful regional and national decision makers. As the community's dependence on wage work increased and San Cosmeros were forced to seek jobs elsewhere, with proletarianization men became factory workers and women became homemakers.

The factory jobs open to men were closed to women. During the 1960s and early 1970s, when large numbers of men from San Cosme were factory workers, as in many communities elsewhere that were developed, supposedly at least, and proletarianized, an ideology of domestication emerged that women should stay home and care for their families (Rothstein 1982).[8] Television, which made its appearance in San Cosme in the early 1970s, carried this message, as did government programs which emphasized domestic activities like crocheting and other household crafts.[9] The exclusion of women from all but the least remunerative paid employment (mainly agricultural or domestic work) and the growth of the domestic sphere (as children spent more time in school and were unable to assist and as housework increased to accommodate more clothes, furniture, and enlarged spaces) reinforced that message and ideology. Families began to recognize the importance of education for their sons' future employment; more boys continued on in school, and a gap emerged between males and females in education.

As Fernández-Kelly notes on the earlier domestication of working-class women in the United States:

On the one hand, by being removed from the wage labor force, some women or their daughters were spared the difficulties that accompany competition for paid work. . . . On the other hand, dependence on their husbands' wages frequently increased women's vulnerability, reduced their autonomy and accentuated their economic strife. (1983, 78)

Within San Cosme, the attitude that women should stay home never penetrated to the extent that it did in many communities elsewhere. Occasionally, I have encountered a woman who said she does not work outside the home because her husband disapproves of such employment or a man who said that he thought a child's mother (referring to his daughter and her child) was the best person to take care of the child. Several people also suggested that if a wife worked for pay the husband might not. There is also a strong tendency for both male and female workshop owners to say that the man owns a workshop. Men and women often define a female owner as a homemaker while male owners are usually referred to as *comerciantes*. When others refer to a particular *taller*, however, they often use either the woman's name or both names.

Perhaps the incomplete or interrupted penetration of domesticity as an ideology is best reflected in the data on gender and education. During the economic miracle, when the male breadwinner myth, as Safa (1995) refers to it, was developing in San Cosme, the gap in education between women and men grew.[10] But in the late 1980s and 1990s the gap began to shrink (Rothstein 1996). In 2001, the difference in favor of men reappeared, but it was very slight (see Table 5.1).

Despite this partial acceptance of the breadwinner myth within San Cosme, outside the community a patriarchal ideology prevailed and continues to do so. Until 1974, the Federal Labor Law discriminated against women. According to that law, "Women were allowed to work only if it did not interfere with their obligations regarding home and children" (Tuñón Pablos 1999, 108). Even after that provision was abolished in most states, women still bore the primary responsibility for domestic chores, and the occupational structure discriminated against women. When women and men from San Cosme relied primarily on subsistence cultivation and the family economy, the national patriarchal occupational structure affected them little. With their entry into factory work (and regional and national politics), men from San Cosme became immersed in the larger patriarchal structure. Through their participation in the labor force (and the benefits their participation brought, such as television and government development programs), they brought that patriarchal ideology and practice to San Cosme. Most women in San Cosme became economically dependent on men and with that, as

Table 5.1. Mean Years of Schooling of Females and Males by Age in San Cosme, 2001

Age	Females		Males		
	N	Mean	N	Mean	Difference
14–19	46	8.84	53	9.23	.39
20–29	72	8.46	69	9.13	.67
30–39	46	6.67	56	7.62	.95
40 and over	60	4.37	92	5.28	.91

Source: Author's survey, 2001

Fernández-Kelly suggests, their vulnerability increased. But as long as most women did not themselves participate in the broader labor market, the patriarchy they were subjected to was primarily a private matter.[11] The growing gap in education between women and men during the economic miracle, women's economic dependence on men and their increased vulnerability, and the meaning of their so-called place in the home all took on a new significance during the economic crisis of the 1980s. As Fernández-Kelly suggests, when women enter the labor force, their vulnerability gets translated into a justification for unequal treatment. Since women are not supposed to work outside the home, "when women work they are seen as invaders of an alien territory—that of men" (1983, 87). Thus, they do not have to be treated as equals.

The crisis of the 1980s pushed women throughout the world into the labor force. In Mexico, women's share of the labor force increased from 19 percent of the economically active population in 1970 to 25 percent in 1979 and 32 percent in 1988 (Pedrero Nieto 1990, 133). During the 1980s, women's labor force participation and self-employment increased even more in San Cosme than nationally. Between 1980 and 1989, women's share of the paid labor force more than doubled—from 12 to 25 percent (see Table 5.2).[12] By 1994, women's share further increased to 38 percent then dropped slightly to 30 percent in 2001.[13] Among young women, however, more than half are in the labor force, and the proportion is slightly higher today than in the past (see Table 5.3).

How have San Cosmeras fared since they have been in the labor force in such a significant way? Why has their overall participation not continued to grow significantly? And why are women the majority of those

Table 5.2. Women's Share of Labor Force, 1980, 1989, 1994, 2001

	1980		1989		1994		2001	
	No.	%	No.	%	No.	%	No.	%
Men in Paid Work	191	88	178	75	278	62	171	70
Women in Paid Work	26	12	58	25	170	38	72	30

Source: Author's surveys

Table 5.3. Occupation by Gender for 15–19-year-olds, 1989–2001

	Women		Men		Total	
Occupation	No.	%	No.	%	No.	%
1989						
Paid work	8	16	18	43	26	29
Campesino/a	0	–	5	12	5	6
Homemaker	29	59	0	–	29	32
Student	12	25	18	44	30	33
Total	49	100	41	99	90	100
1994						
Paid work	24	50	18	56	42	54
Campesino/a	0	–	9	28	9	10
Homemaker	14	29	0	–	14	17
Student	10	21	5	16	15	19
Total	48	100	32	100	80	100
2001						
Paid work	21	57	21	51	42	54
Campesino/a	0	–	3	7	3	4
Homemaker	5	14	0	–	5	6
Student	11	30	17	41	28	36
Total	37	101	41	99	78	100

Source: Author's surveys

at the bottom of the local garment industry? To answer these questions it is important to look more closely at the Mexican occupational structure and the possibilities for mobility for San Cosme's working-class residents.

Gender, Class, and Social Mobility in San Cosme

During the 1960s and 1970s, some men and then women from San Cosme were able to experience some social mobility. Between 1940 and 1970, what Escobar Latapi and Roberts (1991) refer to as the new middle class grew rapidly. Much of this growth was due to the growth of state employment, especially in health and education. As Escobar Latapi and Roberts point out, "There was a degree of upward social mobility for those children of workers and petty merchants who acquired the right credentials" (1991, 101). By 1989, almost a fifth of the women from San Cosme and 6 percent of the men in the paid labor force were professionals (Rothstein 1999, Table 1). In the 1990s, however, there was a decline in the proportion of professionals.[14] Although the decline was due in part to the increased participation in paid labor by both men and women, it was also a consequence of the decrease in public sector employment that reduced the possibilities for mobility, especially for the sons and daughters of the working class. Even when a larger proportion of women were professionals, it should be noted that they were mostly teachers or nurses who earned less than male factory workers.

Although their social mobility through professional employment is also now more limited, men still have had some access to better-paying factory jobs in the automobile or chemical sectors, for example, at Volkswagen in Puebla. Men also have commercial opportunities that are more lucrative than those for women, such as working as garment contractors or brokers who distribute *maquila* or as self-employed taxi drivers. Since women's access to better-paying jobs, bonuses, and severance pay is less than men's, they usually have less capital to invest in a business of their own. Therefore, women's commercial activities are those that require less capital and are less lucrative, such as selling tacos or cooked corn in front of their houses or on the central plaza.

Even before the crisis, and before women's increased participation as workers, the Mexican labor market was not growing sufficiently to incorporate the growing labor force. Since the crisis, the problem has been exacerbated. Between 1980 and 1996, the economically active population increased by seventeen million, but the economy created only two million new jobs (Dussel Peters 1998, 36).

Not only are not enough jobs being created, the sector in which jobs were created during the 1980s and early 1990s were the *maquiladoras*. The export-oriented *maquiladora* apparel sector, for example, grew at about 10 percent annually during the late 1980s and in the 1990s even more rapidly (Gereffi 1997, 61). As numerous studies have shown, most employment in the *maquiladora* sector is low waged, insecure, and offers little mobility (Fernández-Kelly 1983; Collins 2000). Not surprisingly, most *maquiladora* workers are women.

It is in this context of national occupational opportunities (or lack of them) that we must view women in San Cosme's garment industry. For most women in San Cosme the greatest opportunities are in jobs with lower wages, either in the growing number of *maquiladoras* in the region or in the informal sector.[15] While better opportunities for women are shrinking or not expanding as rapidly as the economically active population is growing, low wage jobs of precisely the kind discussed by Fernández-Kelly, which build on and reinforce an ideology of women as a temporary labor force (who are really supposed to be at home), have been expanding.

In the 1980s, women from San Cosme, such as Doña Gloria, worked in *maquiladoras* making women's undergarments, hosiery, handbags, and appliances for export to the United States. Today, however, despite the significant growth of *maquiladoras* and export manufacturing in the region, San Cosmeras are much more likely to work in the local *talleres*—their own or others—than in these factories. In the neighboring community of Papalotla, a new industrial corridor has developed with the aid of the state that employs over four thousand people, most of them women, in thirteen garment factories ranging in size from forty-five workers to more than twenty-five hundred. All but one (opened in 1986) were established since the 1990s.[16] Most young women in San Cosme prefer to work in the local *talleres* rather than in these larger garment or other factories in the surrounding communities. In one factory in Papalotla that employs over 220 people, 90 percent of whom are women, the administrator reported that only two of the workers are from San Cosme. Another garment factory there, a *maquiladora*, employs over three thousand workers, most of them women, but only a few women from San Cosme have worked there.

Some San Cosmeras do work in factories in the region, but they are very few. In the community survey conducted in 2001, only four were reported working in factories (see Table 5.4). Each of the four

Table 5.4. Occupations of Women and Men in San Cosme, 2001 (12 and over)

	Women		Men		Total	
	No.	%	No.	%	No.	%
Factory Workers	4	.7	38	13.6	42	7.6
Taller Workers (not including *taller* owners*)	32	12.1	25	9.0	57	10.5
Comerciantes (including *taller* owners*)	16	6.1	57	20.4	73	13.4
Professionals	9	3.4	7	2.5	16	2.9
Others (non-professional)	10	3.8	44	15.8	54	10.0
Campesinos/as	9	3.4	73	26.2	82	15.0
Homemakers	160	60.4	0	–	160	29.4
Students	25	9.4	35	12.5	60	11.0
Total	265	99.3	279	100.0	544	99.8

*Owners are only those who were reported as owners. People living in homes with an owner or owners were not considered owners unless they were reported as owners.

Source: Author's survey

had worked in the same factory for at least four years. In two cases the women worked in the same factory as their husbands. Women in San Cosme say the wages are the same in the factories as in the *talleres.* If they work in San Cosme, however, they do not have to spend money on carfare or meals because they can eat at home. They also seem to prefer the more paternalistic style of labor control in the *talleres.*[17]

While more women work in local workshops than in *maquiladoras,* however, here too there are preferences. Older women are reluctant to work in the workshops, unless it is their family's workshop. Most of the workers working for others are young, unmarried women. Often they are working for a relative or neighbor. If their own family has a *taller,* women may have less choice. But women from better-off families often withdraw from full-time workshop participation. The larger workshops seem to be keeping their daughters and sons in school and relying on their (unpaid) labor only when they are short of workers. Older women who have family responsibilities work primarily in *talleres* in their own homes (their own or that of a son or other relative), do homework, engage in another commercial activity, such as vending, or are homemakers. Even in their own homes, if they can afford not to work in the workshop, many do not. Older women rarely work in someone else's *taller* unless they are very poor, not interested in investing in the machines, and/or are very fast and can work at a piece rate that enables them to earn more.

In sum, the options for most women in San Cosme are not very good. In the 1980s during the economic crisis, women in San Cosme, like women elsewhere, increased their labor force participation significantly, especially by working in regional factories. Among those fifteen to nineteen years old, labor force participation is still quite high; 57 percent are engaged in paid work. Many of them are still in school and hope to do something else in the future. Older women, though many of them have been in the labor force, are not likely to continue working for pay unless they are more educated or they engage in home-based work or commercial activity.

Men are not any more likely than women to be professionals, and since more are in the labor force, a lower proportion of men are professionals. Additionally, as Standing (1999) among others has pointed out, men's work has become feminized (either their work has been given to women or their jobs have the characteristics of women's work—low pay, insecurity, and no mobility) so that men's options are becoming more like women's. But men do still have possibilities in some better-paying factories, such as Volkswagen.[18] There, as well as elsewhere, the men's jobs usually pay more than those that women have. This may enable them also to enter more lucrative commercial activities.[19]

Even in the local *talleres,* the jobs that men are more likely to get, such as cutting, tend to pay more. Despite their being able to earn more in the local *talleres,* fewer men than women work in *talleres* unless they are owners. Since those who own or run a *taller* are always at least a male-female pair, as many women as men are owners or managers of them. But because they have some better alternatives, fewer men (and a much lower proportion of the economically active population) are *taller* workers, and the proportion of owners among men is higher (see Table 5.4).[20]

In this way, women predominate in the *taller* workforce. In addition, only women do home work and, although it is difficult to measure, women are more likely also to do unpaid work in the garment workshops. Ironically, women's domestic responsibilities, which exclude them from the labor force, are also less valued, so that when garment demand increases, homemakers (and children and other unemployed persons) are called upon (usually without pay) to fill in. For some this means extensive unpaid work in a family *taller.*

Thus, women play their greatest and most significant role at the bottom, as low paid or unpaid workers in the workshops or as domestic workers for the more successful owners whom they help to have their more egalitarian marriages. These mostly young women, usually from San Cosme, but sometimes from poorer surrounding communities, have little education (60 percent have six years or less), little access to capital, and few job alternatives. The pay even for experienced workers is low. In 1997, a woman who had almost four years of experience working for the same workshop was earning twenty-five pesos a day (about $3) for working from seven to four, with a half hour off for lunch, six days a week. She changed jobs to get higher pay by working at a piece rate. At seventy *centavos* apiece, making fifty to sixty pieces in an eight-hour day, she boosted her pay significantly to about thirty-six pesos a day. Although her move meant a significant increase, it was still much less than the two and a half times the minimum wage, or sixty-six pesos a day, required at the time to provide for an average family (Muñoz & Calderón, 1997). By 2001, wages had increased to about eighty pesos a day (about $7). But the cost of living had increased more.[21] None of the workers has benefits, and even experienced and better-paid workers are expected to work long hours when demand is great and are let go when demand is slow. Along with unpaid workers, mostly women and girls who are at home and available, these low-paid workers form the base of small-scale garment production.

Women workers, although they are exploited the most, are not the only ones exploited in the garment industry. The number of young men in the *taller* workforce is increasing. Owners, especially of the smaller workshops, are also exploited. They too often work very long hours and set a rapid work pace for workers to follow.[22] One small family workshop relied on the unpaid labor of the husband, the wife, and an eighteen-year-old cousin of the wife's who had lived and worked with them for three years. The husband said they assembled about a thousand T-shirts a week, for which they were paid three and a half pesos per piece.[23] They usually work six days a week, ten to twelve hours a day. Except for the cut pieces for the T-shirts, they supply all of the materials, tools, electricity, and the three different machines they bought on the installment plan (a collar sewing machine, an *over*, and a *recta*). When asked if he wanted his three-year-old son to go into the business, he said no, the work was *pesado* (heavy). Although some, like Doña Gloria's, appear to be doing well, most workshops are small—fewer than five workers and increasingly doing *maquila* rather than independent production. More and more they are doing *maquila* for San Cosme's larger producers. Thus, while the larger independent producers may protect themselves from market adversity by subcontracting, these small *maquila* workshops are in a very precarious position.

Even the owners—whether large or small—face a very volatile apparel market. Those who own the larger workshops, like petty commodity producers in general, have "an exaggerated form of instability" (Bernstein 2001, 30). Studies elsewhere suggest that the survival rate among small-scale factories, especially garment factories, is very low (DGBAS cited by Hsiung 1996, 68; Blim 1992). Although the larger independent workshop owners are now, like Bernstein's "rich peasants," in a position to pursue diverse accumulation strategies (including subcontracting to San Cosme's less successful workshops), which may protect them when the volatile garment market changes, they may fall from grace (to borrow the phrase applied by anthropologist Kathleen Newman to downwardly mobile New Jerseyites) if their strategies are not diverse enough. Middle producers (those with five to fifteen workers), like middle peasants, who are able to meet the demands of simple reproduction but not to participate in expanded reproduction as rich peasants do, are very vulnerable even to temporary fluctuations in the market. Small producers (less than five workers) and those who work for others, like poor peasants who "struggle to merely reproduce" (Bernstein 2001, 30), may not be able to withstand even temporary fluctuations. As one woman with a two-person *maquila* workshop suggested, when times are rough, they eat just corn.

Not Cheap Enough

That San Cosmeros/as have been able to endure the volatile garment market is due in large part to their multiple income strategies, which subsidize garment production and also to their flexibility regarding production. They change what they produce, how they produce, for whom, and how much very often. Although they cannot control the unstable apparel market, they have adapted to that market to survive its volatility.

What they cannot control, however, is what has been called the "race to the bottom," the competition in which workers, communities, and countries cut labor, environmental, and social costs to attract mobile capital (Brecher & Costello 1994). Because of the relatively low skill and capital requirements, garment production is easily moved. Many retailers

and contractors who formerly sought garments in Mexico City or Guadalajara have now left these cities in search of cheaper labor (Alonso 1984;
Escobar Latapi & Martinez Castellanos 1991). Others, as a *Wall Street
Journal* article points out, roam the world like Marco Polos, looking for
cheaper production or unused quotas (cited by Waldinger 1986, 82).[24]

Although San Cosme's producers generally do not produce for the
international market, as national markets are increasingly invaded by international production, San Cosmeros/as are affected by that market
and by the global search for lower costs. Increasingly, the garments sold
at regional markets or at very large, working-class, discount retailers
such as Wal-Mart, with which they may have to compete, come from
Asia or elsewhere in Latin America or the Caribbean. Globalization—
especially the free trade which brought them cheaper textiles, initially
from the United States and increasingly now also from Asia, and machinery and eliminated the midsized national garment producers whose
economic space they now occupy—brought San Cosmeros/as into garment production, but it may also push them out of it. To understand
what San Cosmeros/as must deal with, it is necessary to step away from
San Cosme and see how the world, as well as the nation and the community, shapes the local garment industry.

San Cosme and the Global Apparel Industry

Many of the important characteristics of the contemporary apparel industry are very similar to those of a hundred years ago. One is that the
garment industry has always relied heavily on sewing and other skills
that are often readily available and on relatively simple technology with
low capital investment costs. Because it is a relatively easy start-up, the
garment industry has always been among the first industries, along
with textiles, in industrial transformations around the world. That also
accounts for its long history of mobility and dependence on migrant
workers and the fact that it has often allowed working-class people, especially immigrants, to experience social mobility. The garment industry also has always relied heavily on the labor, often hidden and unpaid
or underpaid, of women and children. Although some of the women,
men, and children involved experience some of the benefits of mobility,
almost since the beginning of industrialization there has been concern
expressed in the media by reformers and by trade union activists that
the garment industry is based heavily on sweatshops and exploited la-

bor. Today, as we have seen, garment production continues to rely on low-paid and unpaid labor. Even where advanced computer technology is used to design, cut, and track garments (and workers), problems of poor working conditions, low wages, long hours, and arbitrary power persist, and garment production is still less complex technologically than other manufacturing. Consequently, it is still labor intensive, and small firms continue to dominate production. Along with these continuities, however, there have also been striking changes. Perhaps the most important is that modern forms of transportation and communication and trade liberalization have greatly accelerated the ease of moving garment production. This has produced a new pattern in which production has become subordinated to a more complex set of capitalist forces than in the past. Buyers of the goods produced in San Cosme—the brokers, subcontractors, informal vendors, and retailers—are looking for production at the cheapest cost. If producers elsewhere—in Mexico, China, or in other parts of the world—produce more cheaply, these intermediaries move there. But the ability to move to take advantage of lower production costs varies. As Collins points out, "Large firms have important resources that allow them to establish *global* production networks. . . ." (2000, 167; emphasis added). The garment industry has become increasingly concentrated with retailers and their "hollow" or virtual factories growing in importance (Gereffi 1994). Because of subcontracting, networking, and the use of unregistered workshops, it is very difficult to get accurate data on the apparel industry.[25] What is available, however, suggests that although a great deal of garment production is done by small firms, production is controlled by larger and larger firms. In the words of a *New York Times* business writer, "In recent years more and more clothing companies have acted like hungry jungle creatures, devouring every small company in sight" (Rozhon 2003, C16). Even in San Cosme, the larger workshops are increasing their share of the market by relying on subcontracting. But whether even these larger firms are strong enough to survive is questionable. How do the strong survive? There is a great deal of new technology that tells producers, often far away, what to produce and tells buyers in schools, for example, what to buy, and new software programs that reduce waste in cutting and that can transmit design information. Large manufacturers and retailers can take advantage of these and other forms of time-space compression, aggressive marketing, and branding in ways that small vendors cannot.[26] Large retailers can also pressure producers to produce more cheaply. The highly concentrated purchasing power of mega-retailers like Wal-Mart "gives them enormous leverage over textiles and clothing manufacturers" (Dicken 1998, 295). Walmex, Wal-Mart's Mexican subsidiary, is already Mexico's largest retailer, with over six hundred stores and 40 percent of the retail market, and the company is planning on opening seventy-seven stores by mid-2005 (Authers 2003; Reuters 2004). Lee Scott, president of Wal-Mart, recently pointed out that the large share of market activity still in Mexico's informal sector suggests a potential for even greater growth than the numbers based only on the formal sector suggest (Gale Group 2003). At the moment, apparel prices in Wal-Mart's Mexican outlets, much of which is made in China or elsewhere in Asia, are higher than in the informal market that most San Cosme production serves, but Wal-Mart's strategy is to constantly lower costs. Their Plus One policy requires that buyers must either lower the cost or raise the quality without raising the price (Cleeland, Iritani, & Marshall 2003).

Neither the most successful producers from San Cosme nor the buyers whom they supply have the resources to influence the market the way Wal-Mart does. Not only does Wal-Mart pressure suppliers for lower prices but its financing practices are adversely affecting smaller retailers that do not offer credit (Hanrath 2002, 15). Its "So That Everyone Can Buy" financing practices offer credit to those with incomes as low as 1,700 pesos a month ($190) (Hanrath 2002, 15). It is the smaller retailers and informal vendors who cannot offer comparable financing who provide the market for San Cosmeros/as. If their business declines, so does that of the San Cosme producers. Only the existence of a large and growing poor population may save production such as that in San Cosme. As the *Financial Times* points out, "With forty percent of Mexicans living in poverty . . . Walmex faces a challenging consumer landscape" (Hanrath 2002, 15). But as Mexicans become poorer, their ability to purchase even very low-cost apparel is further stretched.

In other manufacturing sectors, technology can be used to increase productivity and reduce costs. Because of the relatively low capital requirements and the labor intensiveness of garment production, labor costs are the most significant factor of production (Dicken 1998, 295–296). With the new ease of moving, variable labor costs have become key in the garment industry. A 1995 study of relative labor costs in forty-six countries, including China, found that costs in Mexico were the lowest (Dicken 1998, 296). Not surprisingly, by 1998 Mexico had replaced China as the single largest textile and apparel producer for the United States (Kessler 1999). By 2001, however, wages in Mexico were three times higher than China's (Iritani & Boudreaux 2003), and China had re-emerged as the leading garment producer for the United States (U.S. Dept. of Commerce 2003). Even though San Cosme produces primarily for the national market, what happens in the international market impacts it, especially through competition from abroad. Current reports indicate that imports from China to Mexico have increased enormously with China's entry into the World Trade Organization in 2001.

As a recent article in London's *Financial Times* suggests, "Mexico needs a Chinese shock" (Hale 2003, 13). According to the author, Mexico needs to become more competitive. More than two hundred thousand manufacturing jobs have been lost in Mexico "in part because of companies transferring production to Asia" (Hale 2003, 13). Mexican labor costs are three to four times those of China, and electricity costs are twice as much. He goes on to suggest that Mexico needs more privatization (of electricity), tax reform, and labor market deregulation. Labor is cheap in Mexico, but it is not cheap enough.

The writer for the *Financial Times* who is calling for greater competitiveness in the global market echoes much of the neoliberal ideology that has prevailed for the last two decades. In this view, trade is the engine of development, and the freer trade is and the more support is given to the market, the greater the advantages for all.

In this chapter I have suggested that San Cosmeros/as became involved in the garment industry as free trade destroyed the men's protected textile factory jobs and the national garment industry. With little competition and reduced costs of textiles and machines—also a consequence of trade liberalization—San Cosmeros/as entered the space opened up by NAFTA. In the long run, San Cosmeros/as are likely to lose their competitive advantage. Their industry has survived because it is subsidized by subsistence cultivation and multiple income strategies that cannot go on indefinitely as land (for housing, workshops, and food) becomes scarcer and as there are fewer new population segments to pull into wage labor and income generation.

In the short run, free trade has significantly changed their lives. Few San Cosmeros/as do not appreciate the abundance of paid work that is now available within the community or the commodities that are now on hand because of the liberalization of trade. Many scholarly and popular analyses of globalization are increasingly suggesting that trade and distribution, rather than production, are the engine of the global economy. Yet, whether trade and distribution rule the global economy needs to be questioned. As Marx insisted, the basis of capitalism is the appropriation of surplus value from the process of production. What role do trade and commoditization assume if we begin with production rather than distribution or trade? How is surplus value being extracted in the global economy? In the next chapter, I recognize the importance of trade and commodification. But I argue that the underlying economic structure of global capitalism—the flexible accumulation and the neoliberalism that facilitates its spread—remains based on the appropriation of surplus from production.

CHAPTER 6

Illusions and Disillusions:
Challenging Consumption Theory

Because consumption concerns what people do with things and how things fit into their lives, the issue of agency, rather than the relentless hand of the market, comes to the fore. In this view, consumption is about how people use things and how cultural beliefs and practices shape their appropriation of such things, with consequences for the wider contexts of their lives.

KAREN HANSEN, *SALAULA* (2000, 14)

When I first went to San Cosme in the early 1970s, there were no telephones, only a few televisions, some blenders, and many radios. Most people had one or two outfits they put on for special occasions, but for daily wear they used clean but worn clothing. Many walked barefoot or in *huaraches* (handmade sandals) or plastic shoes. Women and older girls wore braids, aprons, and traditional *rebozos* (shawls made of sturdy cotton) in which they often carried bundles or children. Men and sometimes women wore straw sombreros. Houses usually consisted of a smoke kitchen (an adobe room with a clay tile roof in which a wood or charcoal fire could be made) and another room with beds or *petates* (straw sleeping mats), a handmade wooden table and chairs for formal visitors and perhaps a sewing machine.

Today, almost everyone wears shoes, and usually not the plastic variety. Few women wear *rebozos* or braids. Only older women wear aprons. Many houses have separate living rooms with furniture (including couches, coffee tables, buffets, televisions, and video players), one or more bedrooms with beds, dressers, and wardrobes, and bathrooms with ceramic sinks, showers, and commodes. Most streets are paved and many have sidewalks. As one man suggested, residents of San Cosme now use cars and trucks instead of donkeys.

In the late 1970s and early 1980s, some San Cosmeros/as who were professionals and even some factory workers lived in or bought plots of land for future building in Puebla or Tlaxcala or Mexico City. They said the amenities were better in these urban areas. Today, people return to San Cosme and newcomers from the city and other towns have arrived. They point to the tranquility and clean air as well as the amenities that now exist also in San Cosme.

Few San Cosmeros/as do not see the changes over the last forty years as improvements. Some people criticize some of their neighbors for their materialism and their preference for consumer goods over education. And some think the changes have not been sufficient. But the differences in their evaluations of change are of degree and emphasis rather than kind. Everyone in San Cosme is consuming many more commodities, and everybody agrees that San Cosme has benefited from the increased consumption of goods and services. But do these changes hide another underlying reality that is not so beneficial?

There has been a great deal of discussion recently in anthropology, sociology, and cultural studies about growing consumerism and commodification throughout the world. Many of the arguments for globalization, especially for trade liberalization, stress the increased provision of consumer goods at lower prices for globalizing communities. In this chapter I question those analyses that place causal priority for global change on consumption, that treat consumption in isolation from production, and that ignore agency in their portrayal of consumers as mere followers of the latest trends depicted in the media. I suggest that the increasing importance of consumption throughout the world can be linked to changes in contemporary capitalist production which, rather than reducing its importance as the engine of the global economy, reflect the increased importance of capitalist production and commoditization throughout the world. I argue that the growing pattern, especially among young people, of stress on consumption and the presentation of self through consumption derives from contemporary patterns of global accumulation through flexible production. Therefore, these new consuming practices and desires must be understood in the context of contemporary capitalism and the constant struggle of capitalists to accumulate profit by expanding their markets and reducing their costs of production. The increased importance of capitalist production and consumption, however, does not mean that consumers such as those in San Cosme simply follow the dictates or relentless hand of the capitalist market. The forms that modern consumption takes are expressions of struggles for some aspects of capitalism and against others, for and against various traditions, and for and against different modernities.

This expansion of both capitalist production and the capitalist market has precipitated what Harvey refers to as a "veritable ferment of opposition" (2000, 71). The varieties of struggle—union organization, consumer boycotts, anti-globalization protests, and nongovernmental organizational networks—and the connections between the participants in these struggles and among today's diverse working class are different from those of an urbanizing industrial proletariat, but the struggles and connections do exist. In the concluding section of this chapter I describe some of the ways that San Cosmeros/as oppose the practices and visions of contemporary capitalism and develop alternative practices and imaginaries of how life should be. In the next and final chapter I develop this point comparatively.

Anthropology and Consumption in the Global Economy

In the last chapter we saw that San Cosme's garment producers are at a disadvantage in both production and marketing. Unlike large manufacturers, brand name merchandisers, manufacturer/retailers and large retailers (all of whom now rely heavily on subcontracting to competitive bidders wherever they find them), San Cosme's producers and merchants cannot move in order to benefit from cheaper production. Nor do they have the resources to create their market. The increasing role of powerful retailers, especially in garment production, and the increasing consumption of commodities throughout the world has led some scholars to suggest that consumption and consumers or, in other words, distribution rather than production, now dominate the global economy. As Gereffi, a sociologist who has written extensively on producer- and buyer-driven commodity chains, maintains, "Whereas in producer-driven forms of capitalist industrialization, production patterns shape the character of demand, in buyer-driven chains the organization of consumption is a major determinant of where and how global manufacturing takes place" (1994, 99).[1] In anthropology, Daniel Miller has been a consistent and strong proponent of the view that consumption has become the motor of the global economy. The problems faced by San Cosmeros/as and other garment producers in the apparel market would seem to support the view that consumption and marketing have priority over production, as theorized by Miller, Gereffi, and others. For this reason, San Cosme is an excellent site in which to explore the complex relations between production and consumption. In order to explain the debate, let us start with the approach of Miller, one of the most influential of the contemporary consumer theorists.

I focus here on Miller because, although he is not the only analyst with this position, he has been in the forefront of much of the recent anthropological research on consumption and he is the most insistent that consumption has replaced production as the motor of the economy.[2] Miller argues that it is consumers (especially housewives) and not capitalists who run the contemporary global economy because housewives' choices in the market in favor of thrift determine production (1995b, 7). Despite this rather unorthodox formulation, Miller, who did fieldwork in the Caribbean, suggests that "some of Marx's work retains considerable relevance to the contemporary Trinidadian economy." He goes on to agree with Marx that "there remains a fundamental contradiction between labour and capital." But, he claims:

> The categories that determine social identity have become diluted
> and mixed. . . . Most workers in Trinidad no longer belong to an industrial proletariat but work in government service or distributive sectors.
> Here their relations to the means of production are not easily recognizable from a portrait painted at the heart of the industrial revolution.
> (1997, 332)

Unfortunately, rather than noting that most workers were not part of an industrial proletariat, even when Fordism was the dominant form of capitalism, and rather than pursuing the fundamental contradiction between labor and capital and the nature of class in contemporary capitalism, where many are flexible workers, Miller turns to a discussion of how Trinidadian shoppers vote for cheaper commodities.[3] According to Miller, they vote for neoliberalism and the policies of structural adjustment when they shop, although the political leaders whom they support and who claim to represent them are opposed to structural adjustment policies (1997, 337).

Miller never demonstrates that any or all shoppers choose "the cheapest available source of international standard commodities" (1997, 337). Nor does he demonstrate that free trade does reduce prices, as many of the proponents of neoliberalism insist.[4] When he talks about structural adjustment, he reveals his fundamental misunderstanding of capitalism and of the dialectical relation between production and consumption. His misunderstanding, however, suggests how we might understand that relationship.

First, Miller maintains that institutions such as the IMF and the World Bank "today provide the key 'global' context for the development of Trinidadian business" (1997, 36). But instead of seeing the IMF and World Bank as tied to capitalist accumulation and its basis in the fundamental contradiction between labor and capital, he blames economists' models for the adverse effects of structural adjustment. Ignoring a whole body of work on intellectuals as apologists for the status quo, he insists that "rather than emerging from a particular national or class interest, the World Bank is a relatively simple expression of an academic drive to construct a pure theoretical model" (1997, 38).

What Miller dismisses is precisely what others, more critical of contemporary capitalism, emphasize. The structural adjustment policies that he thinks derive simply from economists' modeling have been more adequately theorized by Nash, Harvey, and various sociologists in terms of corporate restructuring, flexible accumulation, Fordism, and post-Fordism. Instead of pure economic models, we have the so-called Washington Consensus or globalization project (McMichael cited by Chase-Dunn, Kawano, & Brewer 1996).[5]

This globalization project began with economic restructuring in the United States in the 1970s when the postwar boom ceased. Declining profits, largely from internal market saturation and increased international competition (due at least in part to labor's successful struggle to increase wages and benefits and encourage the growth of a welfare state), led many corporations to restructure, usually by closing and/or downsizing their facilities. This was often accompanied by relocation to less developed regions of the world where wages were lower and by the casualization of labor, involving more part-time employment and subcontracting. The initial focus was on corporate restructuring, but in the 1980s and 1990s restructuring extended to state expenditures with cutbacks in government spending on health, education, and welfare.

In the United States and other advanced capitalist countries such as Great Britain, the impetus for restructuring came from within: from corporations, conservative politicians, and conservative voters. In most of the developing world, the impetus came from the advanced capitalist countries via the IMF and World Bank.[6] During the postwar boom that lasted until the early 1970s, many developing countries, like Mexico, in response both to external influences and internal demands from those who wanted improved living conditions as well as those who preferred support for capital accumulation, embarked on the path of development. They invested in infrastructure, industry, and commercial agriculture and followed Keynesian policies that favored state involvement in managing the economy and promoting full employment. Developing countries financed much of this development with foreign investment and loans from foreign banks and international agencies. As interest rates rose and the prices of their exports, such as oil, declined in the 1970s, many developing countries could not service their debts. In developing country after country, the IMF and the World Bank agreed to make more loans under the condition that these countries agree to economic restructuring by participating in structural adjustment programs (SAPs), which called for cuts in government spending, especially on health, education, and welfare (often under austerity programs that controlled wages and reduced government subsidies such as those for workers' food and transportation), privatization, and the liberalization of trade.

Although corporations from the developed world had begun moving production offshore before the imposition of structural adjustment programs, SAPs accelerated the process. In Mexico, for example, as we saw in Chapter 2, prior to the economic crisis and structural adjustment of the 1980s, many U.S. companies had begun producing in free trade zones in northern Mexico. But the real growth in the *maquiladora* sector came after the Mexican economic crisis in 1982. In fact, during the 1980s this was the only sector that grew in Mexico. Foreign companies continue to dominate Mexico's growth sectors.[7]

In the 1990s and today we hear less about structural adjustment policies and more about trade liberalization and global flows of technology, ideas, commodities, capital, and people, or what is increasingly referred to as globalization. It is important to remember that this growth in commodities flowing around the world is accompanied by flowing capital (increasingly finance capital) and was initiated because of the problems capitalists in the North faced in production and profits. It was this crisis in capitalism that created the conditions and set the stage for globalization and consumerism.

The garment industry in San Cosme arose as a consequence of Mexico's economic restructuring, especially because of trade liberalization. Economic restructuring opened Mexico to huge flows of foreign capital and commodities, initially largely from the United States and now also from Europe and Asia as well. Among the effects of trade liberalization was that San Cosmeros lost their factory jobs in the national textile industry. But it also brought about the decline of the national garment industry which, like the textile industry, could not compete with foreign imports. A variety of factors, including their proximity to the Federal District and the development of an adequate infrastructure during the 1960s and 1970s, enabled San Cosmeros/as to enter that space. More San Cosmeros/as are now involved in commodity production than ever before—as garment workers, owners, and merchants. Related to this increased participation in commodity production has been a marked increase also in commodity consumption. Commodities are cheaper, and participation in their production has necessitated some increase in their consumption (for example, the purchasing of tortillas when homemakers become wage workers) and provided more disposable income for some segments of the population: youth, people in households with multiple income generators, and the more prosperous community members.

At first glance, it would seem that this consumerism does help shape the global economy. Most consumers in San Cosme, as elsewhere, choose cheaper products made by Chinese workers, for example, over similar, more expensive items made by Mexican or U.S. workers. Consumers have benefited from the liberalization of trade and the flow of capital of globalization. Consumers in the United States, for example, paid 2 percent less for a typical item of clothing in 1997 than they did in 1994 (Clark 1997, 2). Many items that were prohibitive in price in Mexico during the economic miracle because they were protected during import substitution industrialization are now quite affordable. When I went to Mexico in the 1970s, people often asked me to bring cameras, radios, blenders, and apparel. These items were much more expensive in Mexico than in the United States, and many Mexicans thought that the U.S.-made items were better than those made in Mexico. Now when I go to Mexico it is hard to come up with desirable gifts. If anyone asks for anything in particular from the United States, it is usually a specific U.S. brand. In 2000, for example, a man asked me to bring a Nautica jacket because such items still cost more in Mexico. More than 75 percent of the households now have radios, televisions, and blenders (INEGI 2001) made in Mexico, the United States, or Asia. In 1989, a year before NAFTA but after Mexico had already reduced many of its trade barriers, knowing that U.S.-made appliances were no longer in short supply in Mexico, I brought a variety of items purchased at a CorningWare outlet store in New York. Shortly after I arrived in San Cosme, I went with some friends to a new mall on the outskirts of

Puebla, about fifteen minutes away. There I encountered many of the items (at the same prices I had paid) that I had brought to Mexico.

Free trade has no doubt reduced the prices of imported commodities.[8] But particularly noticeable in the 1990s and at the turn of the century were not only reduced prices but also a tremendous increase in commodity consumption beyond what would be expected just from the cost savings. In the early 1970s there were a few small stores that sold eggs, dried chiles, some vegetables, rolls, and a few packaged items such as canned sardines, soda, beer, chocolate bars, packaged chicken broth, soap and detergent. Today, there is little that one cannot buy in San Cosme, and people go regularly to Puebla and elsewhere to shop. Thirty years ago, as indicated in Chapter 3, most people relied heavily on their own subsistence production, especially of corn but also of squash, beans, and chickens. Meat was sold only on Saturday and Sunday. In 1971 I went to a local store and asked the proprietor if she would sell me tortillas on a daily basis. Her response was amusement that I wanted to purchase tortillas. Today, respondents in over a quarter of the households (26 percent) said they regularly buy tortillas, and most families consume many purchased food items. Meat is available daily, and one can buy chicken parts as well as live chickens every day. Roast chickens are also sold all the time and prepared foods, such as corn on the cob, tacos, *chalupas,* and other snacks are available most afternoons and evenings.

Men's, women's, and children's clothing and shoes are sold within the community. There is a furniture store, several stores that sell household items, pharmacies, and an appliance store. There are a number of stationery stores, and in 2001 two stores opened that rented computers and Internet access. But how do people use things and how, as Hansen suggests, do cultural beliefs and practices shape their appropriation?

Capitalist Consumption: Two Approaches

The United States has long been recognized as a consumer society. Increasingly also now, the kind of consumerism that characterized the United States is being described in Europe and communities such as San Cosme throughout the developing world (Storper 2000, 391–392). Until recently, anthropology, along with other disciplines, generally ignored consumption. In the late 1970s and mid-1980s, Douglas and Isherwood (1979) and Bourdieu (1984) published seminal writings on the subject (Miller 1995a). Theirs stimulated other work in many fields, including sociology, marketing, history, economics, psychology, and cultural studies, as well as anthropology (Miller 1995a). Initially, most studies of consumption focused on the North, but in the 1980s and 1990s, as commoditization spread and intensified, anthropological concern with consumption in the developing world increased.[9]

Two approaches are generally used in discussions of both the North and the South. The first, influenced especially by Bourdieu, Baudrillard, and Douglas and Isherwood, focuses on the meaning of the goods consumed and stresses objects as symbols. According to this view, as capitalism expands into previously less penetrated areas, land and labor are commodified and objects are taken out of their social contexts or "de-socialized" (Mauss cited by Carrier 1995, 30). De-socialized objects can then take on abstract value. According to Carrier:

> In commodity relations the objects are alienated from the transactors; they are not especially associated with a transactor, nor do they speak of any past or future relationships between transactors. Instead, objects are treated solely as bearers of abstract value or utility. (1995, 20)

As impersonal bearers of abstract value, objects are capable of being invested with symbolic meaning and then, by possessing the object, the possessor can appropriate that meaning. As Baudrillard points out:

> In capitalist societies, consumption should be understood as a process in which only the signs attached to goods are actually consumed, and hence . . . commodities are not valued for their use but understood as possessing a meaning that is determined by their position in a self-referential system of signifiers. (cited by Campbell 1995, 103)

In other words, in capitalist societies, consumers consume signs. It is this symbolic aspect that has attracted most of the recent anthropological attention on consumption and identity construction. Recent anthropological studies link the consumption of new commodities to perceptions of modernity and show how various segments of the population construct new identities through consumption. For Friedman, for example, who wants to "partly dissolve the category of consumption into the broader strategies of self-definition and self-maintenance" (1994, 168), consumption is "a particular means of creating an identity" (1994, 169).[10]

The second approach, utilized by Mintz (1985), Heyman (1991), Carrier (1995), Schneider (1994), Roseberry (1996), Carrier and Heyman (1997) and K. Hansen (2000), follows Marx and looks at the connections between production and consumption. More recently, there has been an attempt to link the two approaches and look at both identity construction and structure. Carla Freeman (2000), for example, shows how high-tech workers in Barbados consume professional dress to establish an identity that both reinforces and questions their working class position. Similarly, Elizabeth Chin insists that "any particular act of consumption is a moment—a snapshot—taken at the confluence of complex social, political, and historical streams" (2001, 175). Although Chin focuses on the symbolic aspects of consumption by Black children in New Haven, she contextualizes their symbolic statements and their symbolic oppression in the broader political-economic structure. Such an approach, which looks at identity and structure, is useful also for understanding consumption in San Cosme.

San Cosmeros/as consume in part to establish particular identities. But what identities they aim for and the extent to which consumption is identity-oriented (that is, whether their consumption is more symbolic than practical) are influenced by the structural circumstances in which they find themselves. Obviously, better-off members of the community are more involved in commodity consumption for practical and symbolic reasons. But other economic and social principles also affect consumption and identity construction.

A Local View of Consumption: Age and Consumption

Marketers are very aware of the importance of youth and children in consumption. Many studies cite indications of the important role of young people throughout the world as consumers. Despite the fact that the subjects in many studies of consumption are young people, few anthropologists have focused on age and consumption.[11] Age figures in patterns of consumption in San Cosme in two ways: Older and younger people have very different consumption patterns, and among younger people, age trumps income.

Among young people, regardless of their family's wealth, consumption has intensified. They are the purchasers of much of the prepared food sold in the community, the compact discs and tapes, clothes, especially jeans and T-shirts, personal care products, and decorative items such as jewelry or music boxes and decorative clocks. Several factors account for their greater consumption. First, although many of the young workers in the *talleres* do make financial contributions to help their parents and siblings, most young people, unless they are unpaid workers in a family workshop, control at least a portion of their earnings. Since their basic expenses (housing and food) are subsidized by their families, they often have more disposable income than their elders.[12] Young people may save for more costly items, such as a television, video or DVD player, but most of what they purchase is less expensive. These less costly purchases are often associated with a great deal of choice. Since, as Carrier and Heyman (1997) suggest, the difference between items on cost is little, symbolic aspects assume more prominence. Young people are also most often the targets of the media and its projections of modernity.

In addition to media influence, the changing nature of the community and their place in it also makes young people the most identity-oriented and the most involved in consuming identities. Young people have been more heavily affected by the dissolution of older social identities. Capitalist expansion and commodification have impacted traditional social identities in San Cosme as elsewhere. Older people have kin, neighborhood, and class identities that are known throughout the community and are reinforced through traditional celebrations and practices. They have achieved their identities through kinship, religious participation, public service, and occupation, usually as *campesinos/as* or *obreros*. These identities sometimes involve consumption. Religious participation, for example, often means sponsoring a *fiesta*, buying a cape and headdress to dance for Carnival, or contributing money and/ or labor for church maintenance or expansion. But these expenses are less individualized and usually involve contributions in cash or kind by others as well. Furthermore, the choice is a matter of whether or not to participate in the religious activities rather than what to consume once involved. The expenses are routine. One can be more lavish by having more fireworks, for example, but the types of purchases made are basically always the same. Furthermore, while a *cargo* holder and his family get prestige for sponsoring a religious activity, what they purchase is not as important as that they sponsor the *fiesta*.[13] The cooperation of many with costs and labor means also that recognition is given to families rather than individuals.[14]

Figure 6.1. *Faena* (communal labor) enlarging the church, 2001 (Photo courtesy of Amando Lara Rojas)

Young people are less likely to be identified with or identify themselves in traditional ways. In part this is because young people are not eligible to participate, for example, in the *cargo* system until they are married. Additionally, because of the changed nature of the community, young people are often simply excluded from many of the traditional identities. If they have been in school, they may not have been involved in subsistence production. As the value of corn declines, corn production has dropped so that their families may not need their labor in the fields. Consequently, while their parents, including retired factory workers, often identify as *campesinos/as,* the sons and daughters do not. Furthermore, a kind of disdain has emerged, especially among young people, regarding rural practices. As they get older, they may show nostalgia for rural institutions, but young people today often criticize their parents' or neighbors' involvement in the church or *fiesta* system as wasteful expenditures. Similarly, they often reject or question traditional kin obligations.[15]

This is not to say that young people do not participate in any traditional activities. Expenditures on religious and life cycle events have increased significantly among all segments of the population in San Cosme in the last ten years. But how different segments of the community spend on these events varies by age. Older people follow an older, less commodified, and less individualized pattern of lower cash expenditures and more reliance on the contributions of cash and labor of others. For example, in the past, and among older men, the embroidered capes used in Carnival were almost always made by a family member, usually a wife or mother, or borrowed from a relative. Although men paid for the materials (feathers, sequins, threads), they rarely purchased the capes already made. Today, many young people buy the capes that in 2001 cost $500. Although dancers (now also including women) dance in groups, representing and earning prestige for their *barrios,* the large expenditure on capes and accessories is also an important individual statement. The lavishness of the costumes today makes Carnival dancing a competitive spectacle as well as a community celebration. People, especially young people, now comment on the novelty and extravagance of the costumes as well as the size of the dance groups that each *barrio* sends. Old costumes are disparaged, especially by young people.

Increasingly individualized consumption is also apparent in a new pattern not yet practiced in San Cosme but discussed by some and practiced by friends and relatives of San Cosmeros/as who live elsewhere. Some families celebrate a birthday or other life cycle event not by giving a party (which has traditionally been a way of redistributing some wealth and maintaining kinship connections) but by taking a trip. I first became aware of this pattern several years ago when I attended a large *quinceañera* (fifteenth birthday party) of the daughter of a friend of a San Cosme teacher and his wife. I was struck by the differences between that party and how the teacher and his family, who lived in San Cosme, celebrated the same event. The couple from San Cosme had a very large party at their house at which they served *mole* to hundreds of people, including many from the community as well as others from elsewhere, especially other teachers. The party I went to with them, however, given by a colleague from another community, was held at a catering hall in the city of Puebla. Instead of *mole,* we were each given a pork chop with applesauce. At the party, two other teachers who were also colleagues of the teacher giving the party, said that in a year when their daughters were fifteen, instead of having a party, the two sets of parents, the daughters, and the fifteen-year-old's siblings were going to go to Disneyland.[16] I was struck at the time by the more individualistic nature of such a celebration in which only the immediate family participated. To date I have not heard of anyone in San Cosme celebrating this way, but recently when the adult children of one couple, some of

Figure 6.2. Carnival dancers, 1972

Figure 6.3. Carnival dancers, 2000

whom live in San Cosme and some of whom do not, were planning a celebration for their parents' fiftieth wedding anniversary, the siblings were divided. Those who live elsewhere were in favor of sending their parents to Europe. The others, including the couple, wanted a party in San Cosme (that they ultimately had).

Age, Wealth, and Consumption

Among middle-aged San Cosmeros/as there is also a noticeable increase in commodity consumption, but it is more influenced by wealth than is the consumption of young people. Even young workers from poorer families who contribute more of their earnings to their families' basic needs retain some of their earnings to spend on less expensive and symbolically different apparel or snack foods. Middle-aged folks, unless they are among the more affluent, spend on fewer but larger items, such as televisions, housing maintenance or expansion, schooling, stoves or refrigerators, used vehicles, commercial investments, animals, and ritual events (including life cycle events and the rituals associated with the Catholic Church such as Carnival and celebration of the community's saint's day). These goods are more costly but less associated with choice and symbolism beyond the decision, for example, to buy a modern stove. Many of these expenditures are a form of savings or investment. Others, such as a stove, are time-savers. Ritual events, for example, are important in developing and cementing social ties for future transactions. Education is an investment in human capital.

Middle-aged and older people, since they must cover basic reproductive costs, are also more affected by the fact that the more wage labor family members engage in the less labor is available for subsistence production (and reproduction). With less subsistence production, people have to spend more to buy what they no longer produce, such as agricultural products. Fewer families now plant squash and beans and even corn. Thus, more of older people's purchases goes for basic commodities, including food, electricity, and fuel.

As indicated in Chapter 5, the garment industry has produced about twenty better-off families. They began with small *talleres* but have expanded and diversified. The owners of these larger workshops are in their late thirties or forties. Their consumption, like that of other middle-aged people, differs from the consumption of younger people. It differs also from less affluent members of the community. Their chil-

Figure 6.4. Making tacos, 2005

dren consume very like the young people who work for their families, but better-off owners' sons and daughters have more clothes that are more costly, more compact discs and other kinds of electronics, and they attend private schools and live in more lavish houses.

Much of the consumption of these more affluent families goes into investments for more machinery, trucks, and cell phones for their businesses. They also spend on their increasingly very distinctive houses that are often conspicuously displayed for all to see. Houses used to be hidden behind a high wall, in part to hide wealth and control envy. One entered through a door in the wall to a courtyard and then through two or more rooms located off the courtyard—a *cocina de humo* (a smoke kitchen) and at least one other room for sleeping. More affluent households had more rooms off the courtyard, including a kitchen with a gas stove and perhaps a refrigerator, a living room, a bathroom, and two or three bedrooms. In the last ten years, some people have been building very large houses that are right on the street, thus showing off their wealth and individuality, in contrast to the former patterns of hiding wealth and difference. Since land pressure is pushing people to build

Figure 6.5. New house, 2005

Figure 6.6. Private chapel, 2004

Figure 6.8. Girl playing with toys, 2005

Figure 6.7. Making *mole* for a wedding, 2001

multistory houses, even houses that follow traditional construction behind a wall often tower over the wall. Whether they are behind a wall
or right on the street, many of the new houses in the community have
unique and individual designs, with pillars, swans, and balconies, which
make distinctive personal identity statements. Their obvious wealth and
difference suggests that even those that choose the traditional design
behind walls may be opting more for security (which includes peepholes
and video cameras) than to hide their wealth. The interiors of these

houses look very much like those of the houses of middle-class urban-
ites, with upholstered living room units, paintings and other accesso-
ries, carpets, and so forth.

These families also spend significantly more on their children's edu-
cations, family leisure activities, and ritual events. At one very elaborate baptismal celebration given by one of the most successful garment
manufacturers in San Cosme, a couple in their early forties, there were
two musical groups, a *mariachi* and a *conjunto* that played a range of
popular music. Four hundred guests were served *mixiote* (traditional
spiced lamb cooked in paper packages) and were given plastic buckets
of *mole* (a traditional dish usually made with chicken or turkey, chiles,
sesame seeds, raisins, bananas, and peanuts) to take home. While their
parents danced, ate, and drank, children played outside the catering establishment on inflatable jungle gyms.

Gender, Income, and Consumption

Gender affects women's economic opportunities and, thus, their disposable income (see Chapter 5). Women's consumption, however, is affected
not only by their disparate earnings. Gender patterns within the household affect consumption and savings patterns. Even among better-off
families, gender affects women's consumption. As Stephen (1991, 44)
found among merchant families in Oaxaca, women may control some
money for household purchases, but capital accumulated for a business
is more likely to be controlled by men. Nevertheless, the women in better-off families have become fairly assertive regarding nonbusiness-re-
lated expenses. For example, ritual celebrations, such as that described
earlier and which are an extension of women's domestic responsibilities,
are organized largely by women, although their husbands play a role in
setting limits for the total expenditure. Although men usually make decisions about larger expenditures, including land, house construction,
cars, sewing machines, washing machines, and furniture, women and
men usually choose furniture, domestic appliances, and housing design
together.

Women's economic control of the domestic sphere, however, has also
given them the burden of stretching the household budget when times
are tough. As studies of the effects of structural adjustment have shown,
women must feed, clothe, and maintain the health of their families de-

spite reduced incomes, higher costs, and government cutbacks in health and other programs.[17] Although the economic crisis of the 1980s has abated to some extent in San Cosme in part because of the emergence of small-scale garment production, the volatility of that business has meant that women must often try to absorb the downturns in the apparel market by cutting corners. They substitute less costly food items, such as *nopales* (a vegetable from a cactus that is grown by most households or can be purchased inexpensively), and reduce the use of processed foods. Thus, when times are tough, women must stretch their household budgets; when the market for garments is strong, they provide more unpaid labor in their own *talleres* or work more for pay to meet increased demand.

In addition to being the shock absorbers for the economy, women also exercise their control by making choices about domestic spending, especially food and household products. Here again one sees the intersection of wealth and age with gender. Older and poorer women prefer less commercial food products. Several older women (of various economic levels) insist that chickens raised in the house (either their own or someone else's) were better than those raised in large commercial chicken farms. Others state a preference for the taste of fresh cow's milk over that of commercially produced milk and for *salsa* made in a *molcajete* (mortar and pestle) rather than a blender. Older women are also more likely to want to serve *mole* at celebrations. Younger women may opt for *mixiote* or another dish (although, as indicated above, they may still distribute *mole* to guests to take home with them). Older or poorer women are also more likely to choose brown soap for washing their hair over the fancier (and more costly) hair care products often selected by younger women. Everyone agrees that tortillas made by hand are better than those purchased from one of the stores that sell machine-made tortillas. Because they are more likely to be employed, younger women are also more likely than older women to purchase rather than to make tortillas and to rely on other prepared foods. Those who are more affluent, however, rely on paid domestic workers to prepare more traditional foods. As the price of corn continues to drop and families are left with corn that they cannot sell, some older women have begun using this corn to make tortillas which they then sell. In the summer of 2005, corn was selling for two pesos a kilo; machine-made tortillas were selling for six pesos a kilo, and handmade tortillas (which require little investment) were being sold for seven pesos a kilo.

Figure 6.9. Preparing chickens for a birthday celebration, 2001

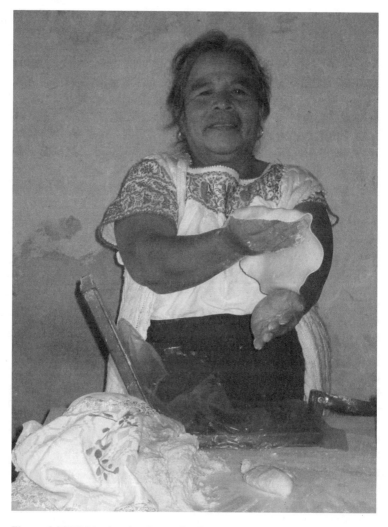

Figure 6.10. Making handmade tortillas for sale, 2005

Consumption and Changing Identities

There is no doubt that most San Cosmeros/as, young and old, rich and poor, are consuming more and are aware of changed identities for themselves and their neighbors. People in San Cosme frequently point out that they are no longer looked down upon by their neighbors. As one woman suggests, today they are more *civilizados*. This is the modern identity that people comment upon most often. Although what and how they consume is part of this new conception of themselves, their conception is more complex than that. When people in San Cosme talk about how the community has changed, they do not stress the big new houses, clothes, or more frequent and more elaborate ritual celebrations. They stress the roads, cars, bus service, and taxis that link them now, the availability of (wage) work in the garment workshops, the higher educational level, the greater number of schools and of professionals.

In a discussion of postcolonialism, Gupta (1998) suggests that a history of underdevelopment leads to a form of identity that he calls "the postcolonial condition." This is a complex articulation of backwardness that informs people's sense of self, "a pervasive feeling of being underdeveloped, of being behind the West" (1998, ix). San Cosmeros/as had such an identity of backwardness vis-a-vis neighboring, more advanced communities, such as Papalotla (the head-town of the municipality of which they were a part until the 1940s), the city of Puebla, Mexico City and the United States. They were told, directly and indirectly by their neighbors, that they were less advanced. San Cosmeros/as tell how neighbors in Papalotla used to yell insults at the women of San Cosme when they went to the river to do their laundry. A woman who came from a neighboring community says that if she had known when she met him that the man whom she married in the 1960s was from San Cosme, she would not have pursued the relationship. In the 1970s, another woman, also from a neighboring community, criticized women from San Cosme for nursing their babies. In 1980, when I had returned to San Cosme for the third time, a woman asked me why I kept coming back. I said that I used what I learned in San Cosme to help me teach students in the United States. She then wanted to know what the more advanced peoples in the United States could learn from a backward community like San Cosme.[18] In the late 1990s, this same woman commented approvingly on the changes in San Cosme, especially jobs, roads, and more schools.

Figure 6.11. Firing up a *temezcal* (steambath), 2005

No longer do San Cosmeros/as see themselves or their practices as backward. Many people are proud of the continuation of older practices which distinguish them from urban communities, such as saying hello in the streets, giving people an *olla* (pottery vessel) with *mole* to take home from a fiesta, and using the traditional *temezcal* (steam bath). Even the young people who criticize their elders' commitments to kin and the church or saints no longer see the community as backward. Today, when people describe how they have been denigrated, they portray themselves as having been *humilde* (humble). Current consumption patterns, however, are only part of what has changed and what they see as tied to their new, more modern identity. Jobs, roads, education, and paved streets are the main characteristics they note.

By stressing employment, education, and connections elsewhere, San Cosmeros/as, it seems to me, are telling us that they value certain kinds of consumption. Additionally, they recognize that such consumption has been made possible by community efforts and change. Although they do not stress their own role in changing the community, it was their agency and investment in the community that led to the roads, schools, and jobs. They seem to be suggesting that there are other kinds of consumption than that focused on identity, which has attracted so much anthropological attention. They are pointing to what underlies changed consumption patterns. They are emphasizing the basic causal processes rather than the often showier but superficial consumption patterns. They are thus suggesting that consumption is only part of a much larger pattern of change that includes not only new patterns of distribution but also new patterns of production. How do they see their place in these new patterns of production? To address this question, it is important to look more closely at how contemporary patterns of production affect consumption.

Capitalist Production and Capitalist Consumption

The consuming identities that many scholars of consumption have focused upon stress individualism and difference. But desire for individualism and difference does not appear out of the blue. It is created. It is these individualistic patterns and supposed consumer concern with difference that are thought to generate demand in the apparel industry and to necessitate the kind of quick response production that requires flexibility. As Collins (2001) among others points out, however, the supposed differences between garments are not really different. Rather, it is an illusion of choice. Various branding and marketing techniques "create a sense, among consumers, that they were making highly individualized choices," when in reality many of those goods were mass-produced (Collins 2001, 195).[19]

Likewise, the surface appearance in some theoretical approaches of consumption and distribution as the beginning or motor of global economic forces is also an illusion. What we need to address is how, why, and by whom this illusion (and misleading theory) is being promoted.[20] If, instead of starting with consumer choices and identity, we view consumption as the end result of structural characteristics, including production, class, gender, age, and history, we can address certain questions. Why has consumption as a marker of identity suddenly become so important? Why, as Carrier and Heyman point out, did the boom in consumption and the study of consumption occur "while the practice of consumption [among so much of the world's increasingly poor population] has been threatened" (1997, 356)?

Carrier and Heyman go on to argue that consumption practices must be viewed in terms of class, political economy, and material reality. But they "stop short of spelling out the implications of their own observations for our understanding of the relationship between consumption and development" (Hansen 2000, 14). Elsewhere, Carrier (1995, vii) develops an analysis that, in his words, Marxizes Mauss. He has much to say that is useful about production, especially about the growth of factory production, impersonal markets, commoditization, and the separation of objects from personal relationships. Unfortunately, however, he says little about class. Consequently, why identity, and not class, has become such an important concern—for scholars and their subjects—is not addressed. In the next section I turn to the subject of class in San Cosme and argue that contemporary capitalism invents new ways of differentiating and dividing workers, including the encouragement of non-class identities based on consumption.

Capitalist, Worker, Civilized, Modern: Alternative Identities in a Global World

When Marx distinguished classes for themselves from classes in themselves, or subjective from objective class, he recognized that class is an identity and, like other identities, is constructed. Marx recognized that common class interests (such as those shared by workers) did not necessarily imply or lead to an awareness of those common interests nor to an awareness that they conflicted with the interests of those of another class (that is, capitalists). What he was unable to anticipate was the variety of capitalist practices that could be used to undermine the importance and awareness of class among workers. Weberian status differences, based for example on prestige, nationality, race, or ethnicity, could be encouraged and made to override economic differentiation.

Objectively, almost all San Cosmeros/as are workers. Whether they are small *maquila* workshop owners (with fewer than five workers), home workers, unpaid family workers, or workers in someone else's workshop or factory, they do not control the means of production or, like most peasants, have too little land (or too few machines) to be in control. They must sell (or, as in the case of unpaid family members, donate) their labor. Even midsized *maquila* workshops (those with six to twenty workers) are basically selling their labor to subcontractors or retailers.[21] Furthermore, only the larger owners have what might be called, following Harvey (2000, 205), a capitalist imaginary: that is, a drive for profit and capital accumulation.[22]

Capitalism's success can be attributed in large part to the many ways it has given free reign to the imagination to make a profit (Harvey 2000, 204–205), but as we saw in Chapter 5, the garment industry today, like contemporary capitalism in general, places a premium on size. Bigger is much more likely to survive and accumulate. The broader political-economic context in which San Cosmeros/as live affects the future of their firms and their own class trajectories. That larger context, especially the media and the state, also encourages some imaginaries more than others; that is, a capitalist imaginary is encouraged while identity as workers is discouraged. Few San Cosmeros/as have capitalist imaginaries, and consciousness as workers has also been undermined.

Young people (who are also the majority of the *taller* labor force) are especially bombarded with propaganda on the desirability of individualistic, consuming identities. Everybody has been flooded with messages from the state, neighbors, as well as from television and other media, about being modern. State programs encouraging capital accumulation are viewed, for example, as established by state agencies geared to encouraging multinational corporations and by means of the state government's propaganda about their accomplishments (in terms of how many such enterprises have opened up and the number of jobs created). Television, the most popular medium in San Cosme, brings to everyone's attention the importance of such modern consumer items as personal care products, electronic devices, and automobiles. At the same time that San Cosmeros/as, especially those under fifty, have had more exposure to ideas and behaviors favoring individualism, consumption, and accumulation, the importance of older identities derived from kinship, community, and class has declined, especially for younger residents. As market relations have spread, kin and community groups have become divided, not only by economic but also by political and religious differences.

Today, San Cosme is pervaded by a more impersonal atmosphere than in the past. Older residents say they do not know everybody; yet, younger people do not even seem to be aware of a change. Many people do not greet others when they pass in the streets as they used to. Although the community is larger, size is only a small part of the change. People used to be identified by family and section or *barrio*. Almost everybody went to the same Catholic church and the same school. Now there are three Protestant churches in addition to the Catholic church. One relatively affluent family is building its own Catholic chapel. There are two elementary schools, a middle school, and a high school. And many families send their children to schools elsewhere. Five different political parties ran candidates for municipal president in the 2001 election. Not only is the gap between the richest and poorest larger, but envy-controlling mechanisms no longer exist to discourage the display of wealth. Today the public display of wealth is common. However, despite this increasing and more obvious economic differentiation within the community, class identity is less apparent. Although San Cosme's factory workers were almost always also *campesinos,* or what analysts often referred to as worker-peasants, they identified as *obreros* until they retired, and they were active in union organization. Although their unions were affiliated with the government through PRI's worker sector, they were aware of the division and conflict of interests between workers and owners.[23]

Today, those who work in the *talleres* are more likely to identify themselves in terms of the specific task they perform, such as *costureros/as* (someone who sews) or *cortadores* (cutters) rather than *obreros.* The absence of overt working class awareness is not unusual. As many discussions of class in both the developing and developed worlds have shown, and as Marx's distinction between objective and subjective class stresses, workers often do not recognize their subjective class position. As suggested above, class, like other identities, is constructed. Working conditions of San Cosme's *talleres* pose particular problems for the construction of working-class identity. Work units are small, usually less than five people; most workers are young and/or women who are new to the labor force; class relations are obfuscated in family businesses; workers and small owners hope that they, like the larger owners, will experience mobility; and the source of real domination is the indirect and invisible domination of parent firms and large retailers. Most workers seem to know only that their bosses sell the garments they make at a regional market, to someone else in San Cosme who sells at a regional market, or to someone who comes from elsewhere to buy garments.[24] Occasionally, workers mention places, such as Guatemala (referred to as "the other side"), Guadalajara, Oaxaca, or Chiapas, from which they might come, but the possibility that buyers (usually vendors or parent firms) are controlling the market and their production is well-hidden. Even the owners do not seem to know where their products really go.

All these factors contribute to the blurring of the class structure underlying garment production. Furthermore, while residents of San Cosme are showered with modern images of consumer items on television, at the weekly market that opened about eight years ago, in the many stores in the community, and in Puebla, there is silence about working-class identity. Everyone knows some families in the community are rich and, except where people think someone has become rich through drugs or prostitution, the families with more money are or were all owners of garment workshops. But despite the levels of ownership (and the fact that small owners also refer to themselves as *costureros/as* or *cortadores* until they get larger and become *comerciantes* or merchants), most of the owners do not really have opposing interests. Even the larger owners are seen as models of what those who work for them hope to become rather than as a group with very different interests.

Everybody (except the larger owners who claim that they are paying well) knows that workers are paid poorly and have no benefits.[25] Workers do sometimes leave to get better pay or more secure work, but there is no mention of unions. If the subject is raised, it is usually dismissed with the (not inaccurate) idea that unions help employers, not workers, because Mexican unions, they point out, control the workers for the employer.

It is not surprising that the view of unions is so negative. Most unions in Mexico have been corporatist, controlled by the state. Even more important, their power to influence Mexican development has declined tremendously in the last two decades. The PRI, which dominated Mexican politics for eighty years, included a workers sector (made up of the unions affiliated with the party) which, despite its subordination and control, did have an influence on Mexican politics. Even before the recent presidential victory of the PAN (a clearly pro-business party), the PRI's power had declined as the PAN and the PRD gained support. With the decline of the power of the PRI, even the corporatist voice of labor has been lost. Furthermore, in an effort to try to preserve their power, corporatist unions supported the state's neoliberal policies, a strategy which ultimately cost them workers' support (Catalino & Novick cited by Cook 1999, 249).

Additionally, both corporatist and independent unions have been struck by an attack on labor. Throughout the world, employers have increased their resistance to unions by threatening to move if workers demand better wages and conditions and by pressing for changed legislation that diminishes workers' rights and collective efforts. In Mexico, employers proposed a modernization of the labor code, which would allow them to deal with workers individually, change workers' jobs, dismiss workers, hire nonpermanent workers, and limit the duration of strikes, all in the name of increased flexibility, productivity, and international competitiveness (García Villanueva & Stoll 1995). Although the Mexican Congress has not yet changed the labor code, the worsening of the Mexican economy in the last few years, and especially since September 11, 2001, has increased the call for measures that, according to the secretary of labor, would promote productivity, competitiveness, skill, and the modernization of the federal labor law (Velasco Contreras 2001).

Given the attack on labor and the obfuscation of class relations in small-scale flexible production, it is not surprising that class is not a strong and overt basis for solidarity and identity in San Cosme today. At the same time also, the market is constantly present and the importance of the market is thrust upon San Cosmeros/as.

Illusions and Disillusions

The growing importance of the capitalist market (among San Cosmeros/as and among scholars) cannot be understood without recognizing the growing importance of capitalist production. San Cosmeros/as are consumers because they have been proletarianized. Without the spread of wage work, commodity consumption as it occurs today in San Cosme and in similar communities elsewhere would be impossible. Not only do San Cosmeros/as produce goods for consumers elsewhere, by doing so the producers of San Cosme can afford to consume what others elsewhere produce. At the same time, all of these producers and consumers are producing profits for capitalists, whether they be retailers, merchandisers, or larger producers. Not unlike small rural cultivators whose cheap food subsidized the low wages of capitalist industry, the smaller garment producers and merchants or disguised proletarians who self-exploit but also benefit from the unpaid and low-paid labor of their workers subsidize capitalism by providing cheap commodities.

Why do these mostly young people go to work in the *talleres* of San Cosme and, by extension, the *talleres* and *maquiladoras* throughout the world? Is it really to be able to shop, as analysts such as Miller imply? At one level, the new patterns of consumption appear to be a way to co-opt workers by allowing them access to consumer goods, as Ford intended when he encouraged the five-dollar, eight-hour day that marks the beginning of Fordism. Harvey points out:

> What was special about Ford (and what ultimately separates Fordism from Taylorism) was his vision, his explicit recognition that mass production meant mass consumption, a new system of the reproduction of labour power, a new politics of labour control and management, a new aesthetics and psychology, in short, a new kind of rationalized, modern-

ist, and populist democratic society. . . . The purpose of the five-dollar, eight-hour day was only in part to secure worker compliance. . . . It was coincidentally meant to provide workers with sufficient income and leisure time to consume the mass-produced products the corporations were about to turn out in ever greater quantities. (1989, 125–126)

What is perhaps most ideal for capitalists today about flexible accumulation and flexible labor throughout the world is that low wages (about $7 per day in San Cosme in 2001 and just two dollars more than Ford's workers in the early twentieth century) are subsidized by subsistence and pooling strategies so that consumption can be used to lure workers with less pay.[26] Commodity consumption can be practiced without mass production and without living wages in either the developed or developing worlds. Goods produced at the *very* bottom mitigate the effects of low wages for workers elsewhere.[27] Workers, for example, in the new *maquiladoras* in Chiapas or Puebla can consume what other flexible workers produce in Mexico and all around the globe, and they can construct new identities based on their market choices.

But are workers simply lured by a few trinkets? It is important to stress that while workers do retain control of some of their earnings, their families need some of their earnings, and some of their families need all of their earnings. The crisis of the 1980s and the restructuring of the 1990s increased the cost of living and decreased wages. The first few years of the new millennium have not brought any relief, so more San Cosmeros/as do need to work for pay.

A closer examination of the structural underpinnings of consumer practices suggests also that workers' consumption patterns are active attempts to shape their lives and facilitate "self-reproduction" (Herod 1997, 16). Among the young workers of San Cosme, earnings are an important source of autonomy. Their consumption is often a declaration of that autonomy.[28] These young women and men were subordinated to the authority of their parents by their need to inherit basic resources such as the land from the senior generation. Today, although their wages do not grant them complete independence, through their dress, music, and lifestyle choices they symbolically assert themselves.

Symbolic assertion is accompanied also with various forms of oppositional practice, sometimes against their elders but more often against employers. The reluctance of San Cosme's young people to work in the larger *maquiladora* factories in the region and their pursuit of more education are among the ways they resist some of the worst abuses of global capitalism. Older women's preferences for home work over working in someone else's *taller* and the frequency with which *taller* workers change workshops are expressions of dissatisfaction with the local form of capitalism.

Younger and older workers also create alternatives by investing in their futures. Until recently, many workers were working towards establishing their own *taller*. The recent entry of China into the WTO in 2001, the failure of many *talleres,* and the increased preponderance of the less rewarding *maquila* production over independent production have disillusioned many workers so that now, instead of hoping to open their own *taller,* many are continuing on in school. Other workers now contemplate alternative commercial ventures. One eighteen-year-old *taller* worker and her uncle recently opened a snack bar. She still works in a *taller* during the day, but if the snack bar takes off she intends to quit her workshop job. Much of the commercial activity that is now so noticeable in the community (which is generated in part by *taller* workers' consumption) began as alternatives to small-scale garment production by former *taller* workers or small owners. More and more also, young men and women are taking the alternative of migrating to the United States. Many return with the money to begin commercial ventures of various kinds or, less often, a *taller*. But in their rejection of being workers do they aspire to be capitalists?

Yanigasako (2002) has suggested that capitalists are made, not born. Although some San Cosmeros/as may aspire to be capitalists, many have an alternative, noncapitalist imaginary. Until recently, communities such as San Cosme had structural mechanisms that fought capitalist accumulation and the making of capitalists. Through what used to be referred to as leveling mechanisms (which, as Dow [1977] and Wolf [1986] pointed out, redistributed but did not level), many communities struggled to preserve an alternative, more communitarian reality which provided a safety net of community aid. At the risk of romanticizing flexible workers, I suggest that flexible accumulation, while discouraging working-class consciousness, may also provide more space for workers' alternative visions of potential choices than did Fordist accumulation.

Class and Flexible Accumulation

Inherent in capitalism is continued expansion. Capitalists constantly struggle to extend their domain while also struggling against workers' opposition. The Washington Consensus and the economic restructuring and trade liberalization that followed from it provided the grounds for further capitalist expansion in Mexico and elsewhere. The recent capitalist relocation of production to the periphery and semiperiphery has often been accompanied by the casualization or flexibilization of labor, involving more part-time employment and subcontracting, without benefits or permanent employment, in both the North and the South. The most important characteristic of flexible production is that the long-term commitment to products and workers is contingent rather than contractual, as in Fordism. Most analyses have stressed the lack of commitment of capitalists to particular workers and the advantage to capitalists in reducing labor costs.[29] Looking at it from the perspective of labor, however, raises the possibility that flexible accumulation may free workers from being tied to particular employers. One might even argue that only by allowing workers flexibility could capitalism have proletarianized so many of them in recent years. Had nonworkers not been given some flexibility, the recent massive entry into the labor force might have involved greater resistance.[30]

To push this argument further, I suggest that flexibility may have allowed the incorporation of many who would not have joined capitalism's ranks so readily under Fordist conditions and also may have provided a more fertile environment for the maintenance of old and the development of new hybrid and/or alternative discourses and imaginaries. The conditions under which flexible workers work—in small units where kin relations often hide the worker-employer relationship—may make working-class consciousness and organization more difficult to achieve. But flexibility may also be less likely to foster a notion of the inevitability of wage labor.

In sum, seeing workers only as consumers ignores the aspects of their consumption that follow more than the dictates of the market. Even young workers who are the most identity-oriented are more likely to be using consumption as a means to assert themselves or to affect their futures than simply to respond to market forces, as some analysts seem to suggest. And these futures, like their present circumstances, are strongly affected by the nature of production and their relations in production. A number of recent studies of consumption have stressed the indigenization or localization of consumption, where indigenous groups "adopt eclectically" new patterns. That is, while selecting some new patterns, they also retain appropriate traditions (Garcia Canclini 2001, 140–141). Despite the importance of that point, these studies often fail to link particular localization practices to such practices elsewhere. Perhaps they are linked by their shared position as alternatives to capitalism, alternative capitalisms, or alternative "visions of economic possibility," as Gibson-Graham refers to them (2000). These alternative imaginaries, sometimes accompanied by movements such as that of the Zapatistas, which attempt to put those visions intro practice, are part of the "ferment of opposition" noted by Harvey. Often these local practices, visions, and movements are limited by not being connected. In the next chapter we will look at the changing nature of the connections between San Cosmeros/as and others and how globalization might affect struggle and opposition in the twenty-first century.

CHAPTER 7

Still Struggling: Development and Globalization in Rural Mexico

Globalization theories stress connections and flows of capital, people, things, images, and ideas. Unlike some observers of globalization, I have assumed that although the nature of the links have changed, important connections have existed among different communities and peoples of the world for thousands of years.[1] During the last two centuries, the rise and spread of capitalism, initially through colonialism and more recently through development and globalization, increased and intensified these connections. In this book I show how connections between the residents of San Cosme and people elsewhere multiplied and deepened during the last three decades, the period corresponding to the development and globalization projects spearheaded by the United States for the developing countries and the time also of my connection to the community and its residents.

In a recent review of a collection of essays on long-term field research, Allen Johnson (2003) notes that such research requires a focus on change. My long-term experience in San Cosme has, as Johnson points out, obliged me to be concerned with change. I would add that my research has required also that I see change itself in a more subtle way, noting its different configurations over time, its different rates, and even the continuities characterizing profound change. Furthermore, a long-term perspective enables the observer to see the patterns that underlie the details of daily life and its alterations, not merely witnessing change and continuity but explaining it as well.

Thirty years ago, San Cosme was a community that had only recently obtained access to electricity. There were no telephones, postal service, or televisions, and only a few buses traveled the dirt road each day. Today, there is Internet service and hundreds of telephones, cars, and trucks, as well as very frequent bus and taxi service on the many paved

Figure 7.1. Internet café, 2005

streets and along a four-lane highway that runs through the community. Two hotels have opened in the last few years, and there is municipal garbage collection for the increase in nonbiodegradable waste. Every time I return I see also the kind of steady and less dramatic change
because of births, marriages, and loss, usually through death and sometimes through migration. I see continuities, too, as people go on struggling to deal with change as it affects them personally, sometimes by
reconfiguring those changes to fit their way of life and sometimes by
pursuing their own way of life despite the changes around them.

Figure 7.2. New hotel, 2004

Figure 7.3. Municipal garbage collection, 2005

Taking a long view of change in San Cosme shows that its residents deal with contemporary change or globalization in diverse ways. Sometimes globalization is used to strengthen existing practices, as when Carnival dancers take advantage of the lower price of South African ostrich feathers in New York and fly someone there to buy feathers so that new headdresses can replace older ones. Sometimes globalization forces them to look for new alternatives—to open up workshops or take jobs in those workshops. Sometimes it is ignored. When I asked a number of people in San Cosme about the Wal-Mart in Puebla, none was familiar with the store despite its having been there for some time.

As we saw in earlier chapters, many San Cosmeros/as used the opening up of Mexico to imported textiles and the loss of their textile factory jobs, both of which were due to trade liberalization, as a time to embark on small-scale garment production that builds on and integrates many of their local patterns of behavior, especially cooperation among kin and reliance on subsistence corn production. At the same time, many San Cosmeros/as resist other aspects of globalization, such as working in *maquiladoras*. The long view of change reveals also that the responses of San Cosmeros/as to globalization often resemble their responses to development. The development policy of Mexico from the 1940s to the 1970s that encouraged industrialization and commercial agriculture discouraged their small-scale cultivation and encouraged San Cosmeros to take advantage of industrialization by becoming factory workers. But as they became factory workers they resisted industrialization and indigenized their own work experience by channeling their new income into traditionally valued channels emphasizing their commitment to small-scale subsistence production, kinship, and community. Small-scale garment production is another form of commitment to the local community. It is based not only on the global requirements of flexible accumulation but, more importantly, on local patterns and conceptions of cooperation and interdependence.

In the 1960s and 1970s, peasant-workers, such as those of San Cosme who worked in factories but maintained their commitment to the land, were often criticized by scholars, development planners, and political activists for not being true workers. These critics argued that peasant-workers did not fully commit to an industrial and proletarian way of life and that, consequently, their politics were not class-based.[2] I have argued (based on research in San Cosme during the 1970s and early 1980s) that such a view of capitalist development relied on a narrow conception of workers that failed to recognize the diversity of the working class (Rothstein 1986). Today, I hold that flexible accumulation similarly requires that we broaden our understanding of workers to recognize the diverse ways that capitalists extract profit from wage laborers and to consider the many ways in which labor power may now be sold.

In the introduction to this book I asked whether globalization is different from modernization or development and, if so, how. I suggested that both globalization and development are best understood as particular patterns of capitalist accumulation that engender different forms of struggle between capital and labor. During the development period, San Cosmeros/as struggled directly and indirectly against Mexican capitalism. The state played an important role in Mexico, helping capitalists (and, less overtly, international capitalists) develop capitalist agriculture and national industry at the expense of small-scale rural subsistence cultivators. Today, San Cosmeros/as continue to struggle against global capitalists (who now include Mexican capitalists) whose commercial agriculture and garment production and sale compete with their own production. Their struggle goes on. But the struggle under globalization, while in some ways very similar to the earlier development period, is also very different.

Many recent analyses have suggested that contemporary globalization is distinct in two critical ways from earlier patterns of capitalist development. First, it has been argued that classes are no longer important or solidarity-inspired groups on which struggle is or can be based.[3] Second, many analysts focus on consumption or the market and explicitly or implicitly suggest that the market (or consumers' behavior in it) drives the global economy.[4] Although at first glance the absence of class identity and the importance of the market seem to distinguish contemporary global capitalism from earlier patterns, I hold that classes and social relations of production do still matter but that our notions of class, production, and struggle need to be broadened to include new patterns of accumulation, surplus extraction, and opposition.

Class Matters

As Panitch and Leys insist:

> Class analysis as a mode of intellectual discourse, and social class as the pivotal axis of political mobilization, have both suffered margin-

alization, although certainly not complete collapse, in the face of the casualization of work, trade-union decline and the fracturing of social-ist political formation, not to mention the impact of neoliberal and post-modernist ideas. (2000, vii)

There is no doubt that many of the more overt forms of struggle be-tween labor and capital and between the organizational forms of capital and labor that characterized both the twentieth century and Fordist accumulation have changed. As Harvey as well as Panitch and Leys, among others, suggest, flexible accumulation, an important but not sole strategy of capital today, has reduced the significance of trade unions. The implications of this are clear in San Cosme. Even the *charro* (PRI- and government-controlled) unions to which San Cosmeros belonged in the 1940s, 1950s, and 1960s have had greater successes than they are having now. Through these unions, the residents of San Cosme were able to tap into some of the benefits of the Mexican miracle—relatively high wages and, through patron-client relations with union leaders, electricity, schools, potable water, and roads.

Yet, as we have seen in Chapter 3, San Cosmeros, like many Fordist factory workers elsewhere, lost their jobs with economic restructuring and globalization. The national textile industry could not compete once liberalization opened Mexico to imports and foreign capital, and so San Cosmeros lost their opportunity for unionized work in textile factories. Not only have many industrial workers lost their jobs but, as discussed in Chapter 6, there has also been a political attack on labor that has weakened the power of organized labor. Those who are still unionized, in Mexico and elsewhere, are constantly threatened with the relocation of their production, or what Ross and Trachte refer to as "capital mobil-ity as a lever of exploitation" (1990, 127).

Instead of being organized Fordist workers, many people in San Cosme and throughout the world today are flexible workers.[5] The new strategy of capital to limit commitment to workers—through part-time and temporary employment and subcontracting—makes labor organi-zation more difficult. The labor force is constantly being replenished with workers who are just entering the workforce (often women, youth, and children) and who initially see their work experience as beneficial. As we saw in the previous chapter, they are also likely to view their work as temporary—a transitional stage before marriage, their own enter-prise, or more education and a professional career. Furthermore, many contemporary workers work in small workshops where paternalistic relations—often among family members—hide their exploitation and make it difficult for them to organize. Like those in organized labor, workers and small owners, such as the majority of San Cosme owners, are constantly threatened by cheaper production elsewhere. They are continually exhorted by employers, contractors, buyers, politicians, and the media not to press for improved conditions or prices lest capital move.[6]

What has made capital mobility possible on an unprecedented scale is modern technology. But while modern means of transportation and communication facilitate the movement of goods and capital, capitalist interests need to be promoted through structural adjustment programs and trade liberalization policies—that is, through political commitment to a globalization project—if capital is to reap the benefits of capital mobility. Without these political efforts on behalf of capital, its movement is restricted. Until pressured, for example, by the IMF, the World Bank, and the United States in the 1980s and 1990s, legislation in Mexico limited foreign investment and imports. Despite Mexico's efforts to liberalize the movement of labor (and new policies which facilitate the movement of business elites), the current globalization project restricts the movement of working-class people, thus providing capital with the advantages of a larger labor pool in Mexico and cheaper undocumented workers in the United States.[7] We see in the continued pressure for more trade liberalization that even NAFTA has not been enough for capitalists. The World Trade Organization and new free trade arrangements are intended to open up additional possibilities for capital mobility. Within nation-states also—as we have seen with austerity programs, wage controls, financial deregulation, and new labor laws in Mexico— what Hoogvelt calls "regulation *for* globalization" has brought forth numerous policies that favor capital (1997, 131; author's italics).

Such regulation (and deregulation) is often regarded as part of the need to cut costs in the face of global competition. Market competition is used to justify policies ranging from cutting wages to removing environmental protections and child labor laws. Currently, many business people in Mexico and elsewhere are calling for the Mexican government to open electricity and oil production to foreign investment, which supporters argue would make Mexico's costs more competitive internationally (Lyons 2003). What market competition hides is how much of this competition rests on low-cost labor for the benefit of capitalists. New workers, especially, suffer burdens that more experienced ones would and do resist. Free trade, which not coincidentally allows capital (but not labor) to move freely, lets capital move production when new workers are no longer available at a particular site, when they become more experienced and increase their demands, or when government cannot reduce any further the costs of production. The process is continuous. Experience, disillusionment, and labor scarcity (produced by many firms relocating to the same low-waged and liberalized site and adding to the growing discontent among the populace with the costs of liberalization) require capital to move to other low-waged sites to find new supplies of workers.

Although many discussions of capital mobility and relocation are seen as simply a problem of market competition, capitalists derive profits and capital accumulation takes place ultimately through the appropriation of surplus value from the process of production, directly or indirectly through finance capital and control of distribution. Because capitalist economies increasingly rely on large service sectors, the surplus from labor power in distribution has become a significant source of capital accumulation. Whether it is in the production of goods or services, however, the basis of profit is the exploitation of human labor by capitalist firms that own the means of production and distribution, or what Lebowitz refers to as "the means of work." Lebowitz argues that "as long as they [workers] are separated from the means of work and need to sell their ability to work," they are dependent on capitalists (2004, 22).

Recent reports on Wal-Mart, one of the world's largest companies, with revenues totaling more than the economies of all but thirty of the world's nations (Weiner 2003), show that its profit is derived from multiple sites of exploitation in both service and producer sectors: low wages and poor working conditions in their retail stores and low wages and poor working conditions among their suppliers brought about by the company's pressure on producers to produce more cheaply.[8] That Wal-Mart uses its buying power to force producers to reduce costs shows the underlying importance of production.[9] Without cheap production, Wal-Mart would have little market control and less market advantage. One wonders also how much of Wal-Mart's retail labor force is made up of workers (and/or their wives and daughters) who have been expelled from production by capital mobility. Workers' separation from the means of work can occur by their having been separated from the means of production in the appropriation of peasant land, for example, or by having been expelled from wage work, which occurs when capitalists relocate industrial production. As Lebowitz points out, "For the wage-laborer, the real tragedy is not the sale of her labor-power; it is the *inability* to sell it" (2004, 22; author's emphasis).

In sum, *class* matters in the sense that Harvey uses the word, as *"situatedness or positionality in relation to processes of capital accumulation"* (1996, 359; Harvey's emphasis), but it has a broader meaning than in the past. Capitalists profit by extracting surplus value from labor in production and distribution. Workers, whether in production or distribution, are often temporary and part time as well as low waged. Consequently, workers, ranging from those in San Cosme to those in deindustrializing areas of the United States, often derive their income not from a single source but from multiple sources. In a single household and increasingly for individuals over time, income sources may range from work in a large Fordist factory, in a small workshop, as a contractor or informal vendor, through ownership of a small store, and by working in a retail establishment owned by someone else. This is the very heterogeneous class pattern that has characterized San Cosme for the last two decades; similar multiple livelihood strategies are apparent throughout the world.[10]

Unfortunately, social scientists, including Marxists, have not always addressed this heterogeneity. As David Harvey notes:

> The central difficulty [of the Communist manifesto] lies in the presumption that capitalist industry and commodification will lead to homogenization of the working population. There is, of course, an undeniable sense in which this is true, but what it fails to appreciate is the way in which capitalism simultaneously differentiates among workers, sometimes feeding off ancient cultural distinctions, gender relations, ethnic predilections, and religious beliefs. It does this not only through the development of explicit bourgeois strategies of divide and control, but also by converting the principle of market choice into a mechanism for group differentiation. (2000, 40)

Flexible accumulation is a new strategy that divides and controls by relying on many different sites of exploitation in many different places often over short durations among many different workers. Furthermore, as I argued in Chapter 6, flexible production (subsidized by subsistence production and multiple livelihood strategies) provides for cheap consumption of goods so that low-waged workers can buy the low-cost goods produced by workers elsewhere and can develop the kinds of consuming and multiple identities noted increasingly throughout the world. The differences among workers according to geography, gender, experience, generation, age, ethnicity and cultural patterns, and diverse identities are real and sometimes seem insurmountable. This complexity of identity and internal differentiation has led some, such as Kearney, to argue that although class is "a formative dimension of identity," it has lost its power "to inform *subject* identity—in other words to be reflected in consciousness as a class consciousness, as a sense of class membership" (1996, 145; author's italics). As Harvey (1996, 358), summarizing Haraway (1990), points out, however, "It is not difference that matters but significant difference." In the following section I argue that important commonalities do exist and may become the basis for class consciousness. Furthermore, while flexible accumulation has fragmented workers, the same communications technology that has facilitated it may also enable workers to struggle more effectively for their mutual interests.

Flexibility's Hidden Possibilities

Especially as inequality grows and capital becomes more concentrated, workers—flexible and Fordist workers fearing capital mobility, discarded workers who have already experienced such capital mobility, and those dispossessed of their land through privatization or forced expulsion—share a common position in relation to capitalist accumulation. More and more people throughout the world must rely on the sale of their labor and/or the labor of family members. Discarded workers who cannot do so must rely on the sale of the labor of someone else in their family. Many former industrial workers in the United States, for example, now rely on the wage labor of their wives, often in workplaces such as Wal-Mart. Other discarded or newly dispossessed workers migrate or rely on the remittances of family members who migrate to sell their labor in production or services ranging from sex work to computer programming.

Although many discussions stress the diversity of the world's working population as wage labor has spread under globalization's current pattern of flexibility—even though that diversity is a source of fragmentation—important commonalities also exist. The growing inequality within nations and among the peoples of the world means that populations all over are experiencing a shrinking subsistence base.[11] Shrinking subsistence characterizes not just the rural cultivators who lost out under development's push for commercial agriculture and who continue to lose land and marketability for their products under globalization but also factory workers, former factory workers, merchants, and many professionals, as well as rural cultivators. Although some households manage to keep afloat and even increase their consumption of purchased commodities, as many of the households in San Cosme have through multiple income strategies, theirs is a fragile balance. Not only is land for subsistence becoming scarcer but workshops constantly close or experience greater marketing difficulties. Furthermore, as the mostly young workers mature and enter the next stage of the life cycle, when their wages or income from a small workshop must support a family, their earlier temporary advantage disappears and they too experience a shrinking subsistence base. During a brief visit in 2004, just three years after San Cosmeros/as had been enthusiastically pointing to the availability of work in San Cosme, I was constantly told that hundreds of San Cosmeros/as, including *taller* workers and small owners, have migrated to the United States in search of better pay.

The increasing inequality and the declining life chances afflicting much of the world's population are often dealt with by individualistic and household strategies of more wage labor, labor migration, commercial activity, education, and so forth. But collective strategies are also everywhere in evidence. Many people are expressing their frustration and opposition to deteriorating circumstances with diverse forms of collective resistance. Numerous indications of that struggle and what amounts to opposition to the processes of capitalist accumulation can be seen in Mexico: the Zapatista rebellion; the formation of independent unions among Mexico's *maquiladora* workers;[12] protests by Mexican *campesinos* against free trade's impact on the price of their corn and against privatization of land, as in the struggle waged against the proposed new Mexico City airport; the electoral response of Mexicans in the 2000 presidential election when voters ousted the PRI, the party responsible for trade liberalization, by selecting a president from the PAN and then in the 2003 election showed their dissatisfaction with the PAN with a record high rate of absenteeism (Urrutia, Cuellar, & Martínez 2003). In what has been described as "the largest protest aimed at a state of the union address in recent memory," thousands of demonstrators staged a one-day strike in Mexico City in 2004 and nearly paralyzed the city (Hayward 2004, 11A). In San Cosme, the PRI prevailed for years, but the PRD gained dominance in the early 1990s, and subsequent elections have been highly contested among at least the three main parties (the PRI, the PRD, and the PAN) and often more.

In the past, movements such as these and the common interests on which they were based were often isolated and disconnected. Today, as the Zapatista use of computer networking showed, capital's opponents can, like capitalists, also use modern technology in their struggle.

In their study of transnational advocacy networks, Keck and Sikkink (1998) show how such networks have proliferated in recent years as activists around the world take advantage of modern communication technology. A labor educator points out that "thanks to the Internet, a century-long decline in internationalism has already been reversed, and for thousands of trade unionists who log-in every day, internationalism already has been reborn" (Lee 1995). Additionally, while the massive movement of people is not new,[13] the maintenance of ties between those in host and home countries—through sending remittances, videos, e-mail messages, and through frequent visits on cheaper plane travel—links workers, former workers, and those dependent on them in geographically distinct places more than in the past. A recent announcement by Citibank that, with its Mexican subsidiary Banamex, it was introducing a binational credit card that can be used by family members in the United States and Mexico (Malkin 2004a, W1) is an example of finance capitalists pursuing accumulation strategies that serve also to strengthen cross-border kin ties among workers. San Cosmeros/as have only recently, since 2001, begun to migrate to the United States in large numbers, but their cash, connections, and ideas are evident in the greatly increased presence and use of telephones and a growing reliance on bank transfer services.

Development in the 1950s, 1960s, and 1970s involved very important changes in infrastructure—including highways, electricity, and educational facilities—that linked people throughout the world to capitalism so that their labor could be the source of additional capital accumulation. Discourses of development rationalized and encouraged the necessary changes, including new technology (especially productive technology for industry and commercial agriculture) and the related modernist ideology of science, progress, and rationalism. Roads and other means of transportation and communication were extended to allow capitalists to utilize the labor of those in more remote areas. These developments supported their efforts to accumulate and allowed the more privileged to communicate and travel more freely and the elite to benefit from the greater mobility of more of the world's laborers. The less privileged also traveled more, but their movement was restricted largely to moving to and from areas where labor (including labor as warriors) was needed.[14]

Today, despite increased inequities in wealth and power, the less privileged also have greater access to travel and channels of communication than ever. Workers continue to move to and from areas of employment and war, but movement and interconnectedness today go beyond that kind of search. Although many people move for jobs, their visits home, those of their kin to their new locations, and the variety of ways that working-class people now communicate produce new and more multifaceted connections. Not only have connections multiplied, awareness of them has increased.[15] In discussing the Batak village he revisited in 1997, Bruner found that "the ways of the outside world now reside within the village and within the *minds* of the villagers" (1999, 475; emphasis added). Consciousness of a connected world exists today among all classes—the less as well as the more privileged. Whether this global awareness is the global market discipline theorized by Hoogvelt (1997, 123–125), in which workers internalize the idea that they must conform to international standards of price and quality or risk losing their jobs to cheaper workers elsewhere or the fear that U.S. wars in the Middle East will have negative consequences for Mexican security and the Mexican economy (a view they expressed often after September 11, 2001), San Cosmeros/as, like working people elsewhere, are aware of the world beyond as never before.

Globalization *has* increased the flow of capital, people, things, and ideas. And while inequality has also increased (including unequal access to channels and control of communication), ordinary people share an awareness of the world and the possibilities of communicating and sharing discontent and mutual interests with others in the same class position to an unprecedented degree. But what messages are communicated? Along with greater contact, communication, and sharing of ideas, global awareness may now be based not only on the messages beneficial to capitalists but also on those that derive from distinctive and potentially more oppositional noncapitalist or anticapitalist bases, such as the Zapatista rebellion or widespread demonstrations against neoliberalism. It is here, in fact, that the diversity among workers may serve as a resource for new visions and bases of alliance. Before turning to this often-ignored potential, it is necessary to revisit the anthropological discussion of globalization.

As I argued in Chapter 1, most anthropological theories of globalization (in contrast to earlier anthropological structural-functionalist analyses of isolated communities) stress contemporary flows—of people, things, commodities, capital, images, and ideas. Where they differ, however, is in causal priority. To reiterate: some emphasize imagination (Appadurai 1990, 1996, 1999); some, consumption and consumerism (Miller 1995a, 1995b, 1997); and some focus on the movement of people (Basch, Blanc, & Schiller 1994). Following Harvey, among others, I have argued that we should stress class relations and the struggle between labor and capital. Critics of Harvey, one of the most influential of contemporary theorists, who take this approach often insist that a focus on capital accumulation gives agency only to capital. Labor's agency, if any, they charge, is only in reaction to capital.[16] My view is that it is a question of levels. If one is looking at the global level (which is Harvey's usual arena), capitalists have greater resources and have been better organized to pursue their goals. But if one looks at the local level, which Harvey (2000) does in his discussion of the living wage movement in Baltimore, the agency of workers is apparent. Class analyses do sometimes ignore or underestimate labor's agency, but "men [and women] do make their own history" (Marx 1978, 595). Neither capitalists nor workers make history only as they wish. Capitalists seek profit, but despite their enormous power they do need labor. As I have tried to stress in this analysis, labor is not always wage labor. Nor is wage labor always viewed as natural.

Anthropologists often make a dichotomy between the global and the local and identify the global by its homogeneity and the local by its heterogeneity (Tsing 2000b, 119). As Tsing notes, "By letting the global appear homogeneous, we open the door to its predictability and evolutionary status as the latest stage in macronarratives" (2000b, 119). Such imposed homogeneity and flattening of contemporary processes, I have suggested, often ignores the coexistence of Fordist accumulation with flexible accumulation today.[17] It also gives capitalists total power to do whatever they want. Elsewhere, Tsing recommends that we "study folk understandings of the global, and the practices with which they are intertwined, rather than representing globalization as a transcultural historical process" (2000a, 344). Although she urges us to situate our theory in "knowledges and experiences with specific people and events" (2000a, 345) and to look at how regional and global groups work together to construct regional and global scale-making projects (2000a, 347–348), Tsing does not see any pattern in the ways in which local understandings and practices might be tied to each other in a systematic manner. Thus, like George Marcus and his multisited ethnography or like anthropologists such as Oscar Lewis who followed people as they moved from their communities, in Tsing's approach there is no theory suggesting what connections are likely to emerge or why.[18]

Tsing's points about the need to study local understandings of globalism and the practices to which they are related is very important.

Her assertion that too often we have seen the global only in terms of homogeneous patterns is an important reminder for anthropologists. The global is heterogeneous; what Tsing neglects, however, is that the local, like the global, may be homogeneous as well as heterogeneous. There are similarities as well as differences. Increasingly, there is evidence that in diverse communities, in very different parts of the world, people maintain noncapitalist or anticapitalist practices and visions, that is, local understandings of the local and the global.[19]

Outside In and Inside Out

There has been a great deal of discussion, including in this book, about the globalization of the local or how the outside is now in communities throughout the world to a greater extent than ever. Although numerous studies have demonstrated how recipients negotiate or customize these messages from the outside and reformulate them with new meanings,[20] there has been little discussion of how ordinary people in these communities not only understand the global but how they influence it: what we might call localizing the global.[21] Unequal access to channels and control of communication means that most messages on television, in film, and via the Internet express primarily the views of capitalists, especially of U.S. capitalists.[22] That is, the flow of ideas originates in the United States, so the U.S. local (or more accurately, the view of a particular segment of the United States) is globalized. But as Inda and Rosaldo (2002, 18) among others have pointed out, messages move also in the opposite direction; that is, "from the rest to the West" and from the rest to the rest. What is very important also is that some of the messages that are crossing the world and mobilizing very distinct populations come from noncapitalist visions—as demonstrated by the thousands of demonstrators who marched in Rome in support of the Zapatistas and what Nash (2001) refers to as their "quest for autonomy."

Globalization allows the less privileged to communicate more widely and more frequently, and flexible accumulation may have a hidden radical potential to affect the messages that are communicated. Most analysts of flexible accumulation have stressed the advantages of the practices involved for capitalists and the disadvantages for workers. We need to look also at the disadvantages for capitalists and the advantages for workers. One important goal of flexible production is limited inventories, so that if the market changes the producer (or retailer) is not left

with stock that cannot be sold. This is the goal of just-in-time production or quick response (QR) strategies. A disadvantage of such flexibility
for capitalists is that a labor stoppage has a much greater impact on the
employer who has no backup merchandise to sell.

From the perspective of workers, an important and ignored, potentially radical consequence of flexible labor is that along with capital's
lack of commitment to labor, flexibility also maintains a lack of commitment from labor to capital. Marx stressed that capitalism reproduces itself by producing workers who see the laws of capitalism as "self-evident
natural laws" (Lebowitz 2004, 23). In this view, wage labor is seen as
necessary for the survival of the worker. The insecurity of flexible labor
may mean that flexible workers do not develop the need for capitalism.
As Lebowitz (2004, 23) argues, "Capitalism tends, in short, to produce
the workers it needs." Flexible accumulation needs certain workers only
temporarily. Flexible workers may also need capitalism only temporarily.

In relation to the people for whom they produce (either as subcontractors or as independent workshop producers for large vendors), the
owners of the small workshops in San Cosme are disguised proletarians.
The instability of their work in an environment of flexible accumulation and the continuation of local practices and values related to alternative forms of generating incomes, such as subsistence production and
entrepreneurship, mean that although they experience wage labor and
capitalist exploitation, their vision is either not capitalist or is a different
capitalist imaginary. They resist working in the growing number of *maquiladoras* and other foreign-owned firms in the region, and their orientation as owners of their own *talleres,* like many of the entrepreneurs
discussed by Blim (1990) and Yanagisako (2002), is often toward the reproduction of the extended family rather than capitalist accumulation.[23]
Many of the larger houses built in San Cosme, for example, serve not
only to demonstrate wealth but also to accommodate the next generation, especially the *xocoyote* (youngest son) and his or her (if there is no
son, the youngest daughter) family. Sons and daughters who have lived
elsewhere for years not only return frequently, they build new houses
for their return visits and for other family members who have stayed or
returned. Grandchildren are sent back from the United States and elsewhere for schooling in the region or to be raised by family members.

Fiestas continue to bring people together and to redistribute some
wealth. San Cosme's streets are now filled with signs for *mariachis* and
stores that rent or sell party items such as tables, chairs, balloons, and
favors. Once, large celebrations spread out from a household's patio into

the street. Today, social halls accommodate such celebrations. In just a four-day visit in 2004, I was invited to eat *mole* twice—to celebrate the baptism of a baby and for the saint's day of a woman in her late eighties—and I missed by a few hours a birthday party of a three-year-old.

There are some better-off families whose orientations may be more toward accumulation and whose celebrations are more likely to be restricted to their economic peers, but the predominant pattern of most of the *taller* owners and other entrepreneurs continues to be a more family-oriented capitalism. Thus, San Cosmeros/as appear to be neither real workers nor real capitalists.

As many historians of labor have argued, workers in the nineteenth-century United States came to accept the necessity of wage labor (or wage slavery as it was seen then by its opponents) because there was no alternative (Glickman 1997, 2). Instead of resisting wage labor, working-class consciousness took a "consumerist turn" (Glickman 1997, 6). Workers (and the growing number of petty entrepreneurs who became workers) struggled for a living wage sufficient for a comfortable lifestyle (Glickman 1997, 25). In advanced capitalist countries, workers came to expect to sell their labor and, in fact, workers in the North today rarely question that need. Wage laborers in the United States may want better wages and/or better working conditions, but rarely do they resist the idea of selling their labor. An unanticipated consequence of the growth of flexible labor, especially among the many new workers being drawn in by flexible accumulation, is that many of the workers being pulled into wage labor today do not come to consider it the only or the best option for survival and reproduction. Consequently, they can imagine a future that is different. Today, few San Cosmeros/as envision a future of wage work, unless it is professional wage work. Most hope for their own small-scale production or commercial activity, such as a store, that will support themselves and their extended family.

For Better and for Worse

Mexico's and Mexicans' relations with the world are more intense than ever before. But relations among Mexicans and between Mexicans and non-Mexicans vary by class, region, gender, and ethnicity. Capitalists in Mexico, the United States, and elsewhere have reaped enormous benefits from trade liberalization, export manufacturing, and financial deregulation. For the vast majority of the world's population, including the majority of San Cosmeros/as for whom relations with global capitalism are now also more intense, the costs of this integration have been great, as evidenced in the growing disparity between rich and poor. Even mainstream analysts have begun to comment on the problems of neoliberalism. Several recent reports on the tenth anniversary of NAFTA voiced concerns about its broken promise (Stiglitz 2004), its "growing pains" (Weiner 2003), or that it is "not enough" (Lederman 2004). Most of these reports focus on institutional and policy factors: they seek remedies, if any, of the shortcomings coming from governments. As one observer sympathetic to free trade notes:

> The short-to-medium term adjustment costs faced by the losers from trade can be severe, and the losers are often those segments of society least able to cope with adjustment, due to insufficient skills, meager savings, and limited mobility. It must be recognized there may be permanent losers from trade due to these limitations. (Polarski 2003, 13)

The residents of San Cosme are among those who have lost from neoliberalization: subsistence cultivators and expelled workers in national industries that cannot compete with international competitors. But despite the obstacles they face, they can hardly be seen as losers. Even if they lose the race to the bottom and the buyers of their garments move on, they have managed to extract something from an arrangement stacked against them—just as they managed to pull out some advantages from the earlier development project. They are working harder—more people generate a household income than ever before. But they have turned their supposedly "insufficient skills, meager savings, and limited mobility"[24] to their advantage by using the proceeds of that work for more education, for greater autonomy for women and young people through their control of some cash,[25] and for the renewal of social relations through more frequent and elaborate celebrations of life cycle and community rituals. They have been able to do so, I hold, because they continued their subsistence production and cooperation among kin and because they have not abandoned the alternative imaginary that such practices foster.[26] To the extent that flexible accumulation allows the continuation of noncapitalist practices and discourages the establishment of a capitalist imaginary—the view that wage labor for capitalists and the consumption it allows are viewed as natural—an alternative, noncapitalist vision may flourish.

San Cosmeros/as do sell their labor and may use some of their wages toward the kinds of consuming identities described among workers elsewhere.[27] For most workers, however, including the youth engaged in such consumption, and for most of those who hire, kinship and community are the objects of their surpluses. Wealth, not accumulation, is the goal.

There is mounting evidence that throughout the world today a variety of alternative visions—to capitalism, to the dominant form of global capitalism, and/or to U.S. hegemony—are thriving despite or perhaps because of the spread of flexible accumulation.[28] Some of those visions are based on magic or religion. The occult economies described by Comaroff and Comaroff (1999 and 2000), for example, use magical means for material ends, and the Comaroffs see them "as intensifying at a frightening rate" (2000, 316). Some alternatives are based on remembering. The legacies of socialism remembered by Nicaraguan women Babb (2001) has studied contribute to the growth of independent social movements. And Rofel suggests that "spaces of subversion" were created by workers in modern Chinese factories by "memories of previous [less rigid and confining] spatial relations" (1993, 102).

In the current postmodernist critique of metanarratives is a tendency to dismiss or not pursue the role of class when analyzing these alternative visions and struggles. Comaroff and Comaroff, for example, see class as having been displaced by other social and cultural constructions despite "growing disparities of wealth and power [which] would point to the inverse" (2000, 301). They go on to point out, however, that social classes have seldom acted for themselves and that class consciousness has always been rare. What they ignore is that the "excesses of neoliberal capitalism" to which they refer did not just occur. Capitalists acted for themselves; they acted as and for their class.

Like Comaroff and Comaroff, I "find it unimaginable that innovative forms of emancipatory practice will not emerge to address the excesses of neoliberal capitalism" (2000, 335). And like them and many others, I see the presence of many "newly assertive social movements" with even organized labor pursuing common cause on a global scale (2000, 335). Few San Cosmeros/as participate in such global social movements, but more and more they are aware of the interconnections between their world and the world or worlds of others. Like many participants and analysts of globalization, they often do not see these connections as tied to class interests—common or antagonistic ones. But like people everywhere, they have always been creative and innovative in their practices and imaginations.[29]

Globalization, like development before it, has not yet been for the betterment of the many. At the turn of the twenty-first century, San Cosmeros/as were very optimistic about the changes in the community and especially about the availability of work in San Cosme. A few years later, however, in 2004, because of the downturns in the U.S. and Mexican economies and increased competition, especially from China, many of the *talleres* had closed or reduced production. San Cosmeros/as were no longer so optimistic. Everyone I talked to mentioned the difficult times that had prevailed since my previous visit in 2001. Although there is still work in San Cosme, hundreds of San Cosermos/as now prefer the risks of illegal migration or, as in the case of a skilled mechanic, legal migration if it can be arranged to Canada and the higher earnings in the North. Even among better-off workshop owners, professionals, and skilled workers, there is concern that the market for their garment production or their labor is poor because labor elsewhere is cheaper.

Globalization has created opportunities for some and disappointments for many. Thus, it is very similar to development. But globalization has a potential not present in earlier forms of capitalist development. That potential is waiting to be acted upon.

Notes

Chapter I

1. Most observers define sweatshops as factories that violate labor laws, including minimum wage, overtime, and minimum age requirements (see Green 1997; Piore 1997; Ross 1997).

2. See, e.g., Korzeniewicz & Smith (2000), Stiglitz (2002), and Willliamson (2000).

3. Even Frank's dependency theory, which saw underdevelopment as an alternative, viewed that variant as a deformed pattern of a single development path.

4. For a useful summary of uneven development, see Blim (1992, 9–10).

5. See Harvey (2000, 40) for a discussion of how capitalism divides and Smith (1997) for analysis of how it expels.

6. See Ferguson (1999) for a discussion of this process in Zambia.

7. See Herod (1997), Tsing (2000a), and Yanigasako (2002) for useful critiques of approaches that ignore difference and agency.

8. See, e.g, Bailey (1963), Barnes (1954), and Frankenberg (1957).

9. See Nash (1981) and Roseberry (1988) for useful discussions of dependency theory.

10. I use the terms *theory* and *globalization theory* loosely to refer to theoretical orientations or models that deal with capitalism at the turn of the twenty-first century, including those that deal with globalization, flexible accumulation, and disorganized capitalism.

11. See, e.g., Appadurai (1996) or Ohmae (1996).

12. For a more general discussion of Africa, see Smith (1997).

13. See Comaroff & Comaroff (2000) for a discussion of millennial capitalists and Tsing (2002b) for analysis of global financial conjurers.

14. See, e.g., Nash (1979), Nash & Fernandez-Kelly (1983), and Susser (1982).

15. In more critical terms, Comaroff & Comaroff refer to "anthropology lite," "fact-free ethnography whose realities are more virtual than its virtues are real" (1999, 294).

16. That Marcus advocates an inductive approach is apparent when he says, "Multi-sited ethnography stimulates accounts of cultures composed in a landscape for which there is as yet no developed theoretical conception or descriptive model" (1998, 86). See Rothstein (1982, 8) for a discussion of the inductive nature of earlier efforts, such as that of Oscar Lewis, to go beyond particular communities.

17. See Bailey (1963), Nicholas (1965), and Rothstein (1974) for discussions of factions.

18. Important early discussions of manufacturing for export can be found in Fernández-Kelly (1983), Nash & Fernández-Kelly (1983), Ong (1987), and Safa (1981). Frobel, Heinrichs, & Kreye (1981) elaborated the concept of the new international division of labor. Benería & Feldman (1992), Bolles (1991), and Sparr (1994) were among the earliest critics of structural adjustment policies.

Chapter 2

1. See Gibson (1952).

2. Between 1940 and 1946 the public sector accounted for 52 percent of gross fixed capital formation (Hansen 1971, Tables 3 and 4).

3. On foreign investment, see Cockcroft (1990, 161); on foreign borrowing, see Hansen (1971, 46).

4. Between 1960 and 1979, total net foreign income on investments varied between $141.5 million and $473.6 million, of which the most that was reinvested was one-third (in 1970, calculated from Cockcroft 1990, Table 4).

5. See also Hansen (1971, 83), Hellman (1983), and Cypher (1990).

6. This period is covered more extensively in Rothstein (1982).

7. See, e.g., Cockcroft (1990).

8. See, e.g., Korzeniewicz & Smith (2000), Stiglitz (2002), Williamson (2000).

9. See Harvey (2000, 122) for an excellent analysis of what he calls "a nation-wide political attack upon working-class institutions and government supports and a general shift by a whole range of public and private institutions towards political-economic practices that emphasized capital accumulation."

10. For a useful discussion of the changing Mexican state that identifies such new functions as the militarization of internal security, see Gledhill (1999).

11. See Escobar Latapi and Roberts (1991) for a discussion of the impressive growth of the new middle class and the state's support of this growth as an employer, especially in health and education.

12. According to the ECLAC (cited by Sheahan 1997, 23) poverty increased from 34 percent of the population in 1984 to 39 percent in 1989 and then decreased slightly to 35 percent in 1992 (see also Audley et al, 2003).

13. See Becerril (1994) and Chavez M. (1995).

14. Between 1982 and 1987, average wages in Mexican manufacturing declined by a fourth (Sheahan 1997, 20).

15. It is important to point out that this was influenced by the existence of Item 807 of the U.S. Tariff Code established in 1963, which allows articles,

such as apparel, that are assembled abroad from U.S.-made components to be reimported by paying duties only on the "value added."

16. Before NAFTA, establishments that registered as *maquiladoras* received important benefits, such as the right to import duty-free foreign made imports. Since NAFTA introduced free trade between the United States, Mexico, and Canada, however, companies have fewer reasons to register as *maquiladoras* (Bair & Gereffi 2001, 1902, n4). For a discussion of the growth of export production in Tlaxcala, including *maquiladoras,* see Alonso (2000).

17. Formal sector jobs have been lost both because of free trade and because of the increasing flexibilization of work that substitutes informal sector arrangements for formal ones, such as in subcontracting.

18. This is the term used by Alarcón González (2000, 56) for inexpensive and low-quality industrial items that are globally consumed, such as watches, eyeglasses, and battery-run toys made in Taiwan, Korea, Vietnam, and China.

Chapter 3

1. Except for public figures, names and identifying characteristics of people mentioned have been changed.

2. Unless otherwise specified, statistical data are taken from the author's household surveys done in 1971, 1980, 1984, 1989, 1994, and 2001. In 1971, every fourth household was surveyed, yielding one hundred and fifty households. In 1980, those same households, plus an additional fifty and replacements for those households no longer occupied, were randomly selected to give a total of two hundred. In 1984, one-fourth of the 1980 households were surveyed. In 1989 and 1994, the two hundred households (with random replacements) of 1980 were again surveyed. In 2001, two hundred households were surveyed. Approximately one hundred of these were in dwellings previously surveyed; one hundred were households in newer houses (i.e., after the 1980s).

3. Many people who call themselves *campesinos* rely heavily on other nonagricultural sources of income. Consequently, I classify a household as *campesino* if the total income from wages or commercial activity is not greater than the income in cash and kind derived from agricultural activities.

4. See Rothstein (1974, 10–13) for a discussion of population growth and subsistence land requirements.

5. Corn prices have fallen recently as NAFTA has put Mexican farmers into competition with highly subsidized U.S. corn. During my brief visit in the summer of 2005, many families reported that they had been unable to sell their surplus corn and/or that they had not planted all of their fields because of the low price of corn.

6. See Rothstein (1999).

7. Men sometimes roasted corn, especially if they were in the fields or mountain.

8. In 1971–1972, the exchange rate was eight pesos to one U.S. dollar.

9. See Rothstein (1982, 52) for a discussion of the methodology used here.

10. See Rothstein (1983).

11. See Wolf (1986).

12. I use the term *workers* to refer only to the factory workers themselves and the term *proletarian* to refer to families and family members whose income is derived primarily from factory work.

13. See Rothstein (1974, Ch. 4) for a fuller discussion of *compadrazgo* in San Cosme. For an excellent discussion of ritual kinship in the Tlaxcala area, see Nutini & Bell (1984).

14. Recent research on transnational migration by Rouse (1991) and Basch, Blanc, & Schiller (1994), among others, has recognized that migrants often maintain strong ties to their home communities, but rural-to-urban migration studies have been slower to see a two-way flow.

15. See, e.g., Dinerman (1978) and Rubinstein (1983). Standing (1999) notes that studies of remittances have focused primarily on rural-to-urban flows and rarely examined remittances as a two-way process. For a fuller discussion of the assumptions and problems with this view of migration, see Rothstein (1991).

16. *Campesinas* also prepared a meal but it was simpler, and they brought it to the fields to be eaten by everyone when they were all finished working.

17. See Rothstein (1982, Ch. 4) for a discussion of household organization and gender relations.

18. For a discussion of patron-client relations in San Cosme, see Rothstein (1979).

19. For discussions of the differential effect of the economic miracle on rural communities in Mexico, see Gollás & García Rocha (1976), Navarrete (1960).

20. Although imports of consumer commodities were limited under ISI, the importing of the technology to manufacture consumer goods increased tremendously.

21. A frequent source of conflict in the community is the use of land for public purposes. In the past in these disputes, *campesinos/as* often received political support from workers and workers' contacts.

Chapter 4

1. Because few of the workshops or people involved in the garment business are part of the formal sector, i.e., registered with the government, people are sometimes reluctant to report their participation. Thus, actual involvement is probably greater.

2. See Collins (2003) for a useful discussion of the overlap between high-end fashion goods and standardized production even when subcontracting is not involved.

3. In addition to complex networks, secrecy often surrounds these chains either because they involve attempts to get around tariffs and quotas or to shield production conditions from public view. The recent boycott movement by anti-sweatshop activists against Gap, Nike, and JC Penney in the United States may have further increased secrecy about apparel production.

4. For a detailed discussion of how NAFTA applies to the textile/apparel industry, see Kessler (1999).

5. Imports from Mexico ($5.3 billion) surpassed imports from China ($4.5 billion) in 1997 (U.S. Dept. of Commerce, May 1998).

6. The 1987 figures are from the Office of Textiles and Apparel (cited by Gereffi 1997, 70). The 2000 figures are from Bair and Gereffi (2001, 1889).

7. See also Alonso (1984), Gereffi (1994), and Bonacich and Appelbaum (2000) for discussions of such peripheralization in Mexico.

8. Mexico has three minimum wages in three different regions. Even today, wages in Tlaxcala are among the lowest in the nation. Along with states such as Oaxaca, Chiapas, and Puebla, Tlaxcala is in area C where the minimum wage in 2003 was Mex$40.30 compared to Mex$41.85 in area B and Mex$43.65 in area A. (http://www.mexicanlaws.com/Minwages2003.htm; accessed May 27, 2004). One-third of the employed population in Tlaxcala is unpaid or paid less than the minimum wage compared with 27 percent for the nation (www.inegi.gob.mx/estadistica/ingles/sociodemcaraceco/car_06.htm; accessed July 7, 2003).

9. The border area, along with cities such as Mexico City, is in area A, the area with the highest minimum wage. Wages are lower in non-urban areas in the interior.

10. This is based on 14,919 workers (of 52,900) in the 66 firms for which SEDECO has data on the number of employees.

11. Lower-end, mass-produced clothing made in Mexico, usually for U.S. firms, was more expensive in 2001 than clothing produced in small garment workshops. As more imports from China become available in Mexico, these small workshops may not be able to keep their markets.

12. Some owners claim to be registered, but San Cosme's garment firms do not appear in national censuses or state economic reports.

13. Fordism, with its large-scale production units and assembly line processes controlling mass production, has not disappeared. But as Dicken (1998) and others point out, new flexible production systems designed to produce short runs of different products are increasingly prevalent in contemporary industrialization. Even mass production has become geared to the production of more differentiated products and the rapid switching of product types.

14. See, e.g., Simmons & Kalantaridis (1994 and 1996) and Green (1997).

15. For a more pessimistic view, see Taplin (1996).

16. For a discussion of the decreasing appeal of education and of professional careers see Rothstein (1996).

Chapter 5

1. Her immediate family at the time consisted of herself and her twelve-year-old daughter.

2. This point is often made in the popular press. See, e.g., Kristof (2002).

3. The nature of this production—small-scale, informal and unregulated by

the government—makes it difficult to know how much industrial production is done in small workshops throughout the world. The recent concern with poor working conditions and the association with branded products, such as Kathy Lee and Nike, has encouraged still more secrecy about garment production. Companies that subcontract often refuse to say where production takes place. As Klein (1999) and Collins (2003) point out, often the workers do not know for whom they are producing.

4. Although men sometimes sew, I know of no man who does home work alone.

5. This is very similar to what often happens with other tasks. For example, if a woman is in the process of shucking corn or removing the kernels (which is necessary before soaking and grinding to make tortillas), whoever is around and not otherwise occupied usually helps.

6. For useful discussions of the advantages of personal ties in recruitment and management control techniques, see Blim (1990, Ch. 5) and Mills (1999).

7. Some neighbors claim that the town also subsidizes garment production because producers use the town's electricity instead of paying for it themselves.

8. See also Fernández-Kelly (1983), Mies (1982), Rogers (1981), Safa (1995).

9. For an excellent discussion of how development programs encouraged men's paid work and women's unpaid reproductive work, see Escobar (1995).

10. According to Safa, the myth assumes that men are the primary breadwinners. Women, even if they are employed, are responsible for domestic chores and child care (1995, 37).

11. See Safa (1995) for a useful discussion of public and private patriarchy in the Caribbean.

12. These statistics are based on what was reported in the surveys I conducted at various times. My impression, based on knowing many of the people in the survey, is that paid work was likely to be reported, but unpaid work, especially if it was sporadic, was likely to be neglected. Thus, women's work, which is more likely than men's to be unpaid and sporadic, is probably underrepresented in my surveys.

13. Unfortunately, the survey samples are too small to analyze this difference further.

14. In 1994, only 9 percent of the women and 3 percent of the men in the paid labor force were professionals. By 2001, the proportion of San Cosme women and men who were professionals was 13 and 4 percent, respectively.

15. Increasingly, these two sectors are closely related. See Beneria & Roldan (1987) and Chen, Sebstad, & O'Connell (1999) for discussions of the links between the formal and informal sectors.

16. I am very grateful to Maria Lourdes Rodriguez for her assistance in getting this data through interviews with personnel in several local firms and from research on regional economic patterns.

17. See Lee (1998) for an interesting discussion of the relative advantages and disadvantages of two different regimes of labor control: familial hegemony and localistic despotism. Wilson (1999, 342) also suggests that home work and family-based workshops offered benefits to women in western central Mexico that the formal sector, while paying better, did not.

18. Whether these better men's jobs will persist is questionable. Because of the higher pay, as Phizacklea (1988) suggests, there is greater incentive for firms to use labor-saving technology and to de-skill these jobs. This can have the effect discussed by Standing (1999) of the feminization of men's jobs. The relatively good jobs at Volkswagen have recently come under attack as the company proposed cutting many jobs in its Puebla factory, subcontracting more, and shifting production to Asia.

19. See Hite & Viterna (2005, 78) for an important discussion of greater gender parity in Latin America, not because of an improvement in the position of women but "because men's working conditions are becoming increasingly similar to women's."

20. Elsewhere, too, women are less likely to be workshop owners than are men. See Blim (2001), Green (1997), Hsiung (1996), Phisacklea (1990), and Ypeij (2000).

21. In 2000, eighty pesos was equivalent to two minimum salaries. Five minimum salaries were necessary for the basic food basket (Zúñiga 2000).

22. Simmons & Kalantaridis also found that "the entrepreneurial family [in rural Greece] sets the standard for the labor process and works longer hours than any of the wage employees" (1996, 10). Hsiung emphasizes that this kind of owners' self-exploitation sets a pace that workers have to follow (1996, 121). Blim (1990, 124) similarly suggests that small firms can absorb market adversity through family sacrifice.

23. In August 2005, 10.5 pesos equaled one U.S. dollar.

24. See Lui and Chiu (1999) for a discussion of such relocation in the manufacturing industries of Hong Kong and Taiwan.

25. Despite the greater use of computer technology to inventory, monitor, order, design, and in other ways control production and producers, it is revealing that data on who is producing what in what context are not readily available. This is shown most glaringly in the resistance of large firms, such as Nike, to consumer activists wanting to know exactly where production occurs so that it can be monitored by labor rights groups.

26. For a useful discussion of the increasing role of branding in the apparel and other industries, see Klein (1999).

Chapter 6

1. Gereffi notes that political pressures from the state influence buyer-driven commodity chains (1994, 100). Unfortunately, like Miller (1995a, 1995b, 1997), he does not examine the role of class interests in state policy.

2. Others, such as Appadurai (1996) and Friedman (1994), operate within a similar framework and disregard production even while asserting, as Appadurai does, "that the real seat of agency" lies in production (1996, 42).

3. See Rothstein (1986) for a discussion of the complexity of proletarianization in both the developed and developing world even before globalization.

4. Although some commodity prices have been reduced because freer trade allows producers to go where labor is cheaper, other factors also influence prices. Clothing, for example, which has declined in price, has also benefited from lean

retailing, in which retailers do not stock items but order for quick production when items sell well. A recent study of trade patterns found that replenishment was often a more important consideration than free trade (Abernathy, Dunlop, Hammond, & Weil 2003).

5. For a very different view from that of Miller, see Harvey, who suggests that globalization was put on the agenda by "capitalist class interests operating through the agency of the U.S. foreign, military, and commercial policy" and supported by many factions of the capitalist class worldwide (2000, 69). For a critique of structural adjustment policies and the interests that encouraged them from a Washington insider, see Stiglitz (2002).

6. China is an important exception.

7. The main exporters of Mexican products continue to be foreign companies, with only six national companies among the top one hundred exporters (Zúñiga 2003).

8. Free trade has also influenced the illegal entry of goods. Mexico did not have trade agreements with China, for example, until 2001. See Alarcón (2000) for a discussion of how NAFTA affected the illegal entry of Asian-produced goods from the United States.

9. The increased interest in Europe as evidenced in Baudrillard (1995), Bourdieu (1984), and Douglas & Isherwood (1979) may reflect the relatively recent growth of consumerism there.

10. See also Appadurai (1996) and Ma (2001).

11. Chin's (2001) description and analysis concerning young people in New Haven is an important exception. See also Comaroff & Comaroff (2000, 306–309).

12. Davis (2000, 20) found also that age influenced consumption. She suggests that the low cost of many of the items bought by young people in China and the practice of having multiple wage earners in a household allowed young people particularly to "spend most of their wages on personal discretionary goods and services."

13. The *cargo* or *fiesta* system exists throughout a community and throughout Latin America. Men fill offices responsible for the performance of rituals, often involving a *fiesta* or celebration for the saints. There is a less-researched system involving women, but that too requires that the women be married.

14. For a discussion of how anthropologists stressed the individual and often missed the importance of the family in discussions of the *cargo* system, see Rothstein (1983).

15. See Heyman (1997) for a discussion of such disdain in northern Mexico.

16. See O'Dougherty (2002) for discussion of a similar pattern among urban, middle-class Brazilians.

17. The gender-specific effects of structural adjustment are examined in Benería & Feldman (1992) and more recently in Babb (2001).

18. See Heyman (1997, 157) for a related discussion of the emergence of a "locational bias against the countryside" in Northern Mexico in the 1920s.

19. For a similar point about the illusion of choice and coffee, see Roseberry (1996).

20. Miller's suggestion (1995b) that consumers and housewives in particular are the new dictators in the global economy mirrors the position of industry

analysts. As Bonacich and Appelbaum (2000, 101) point out about an analysis by Standard & Poor's of textiles and apparel, the changes in retailing are placed at the feet of the consumer.

21. Portes & Hoffman (2003, 51), following ECLAC, consider owners of firms with more than five workers as part of the capitalist class, but they suggest that firms with five to twenty persons are probably not "true capitalists." By Mexican government categories, which classify producers with 0–15 workers as microfirms, 16–100 as small, 100–250 as medium, and over 250 as large, even San Cosme's largest producers (between 25 and 50 workers) are small (Rivero & Aguilar 1994).

22. See also Yanagisako (2002, Ch. 6) for a discussion of diverse ideologies—including capitalist and noncapitalist imaginaries—among the bourgeoisie in Italy.

23. For a discussion of class in San Cosme in the 1980s and a critique of the idea that worker-peasants were not true workers, see Rothstein (1986).

24. Collins (2002, 152) also found that workers in Aguascalientes "did not know the name of the firm for which they were producing sweatshirts, where it was located, or who ran it."

25. Larger workshops offer more steady employment and sometimes, if they pay by the piece, may enable an experienced worker to earn more.

26. Freeman (2000) also notes that what enables Barbadian women to be modern consumers of professional attire is that they supplement their wage labor with participation in the informal economy as suitcase traders.

27. I am grateful to an anonymous reader for bringing this out clearly.

28. See Mills (1999) for a discussion of employment, consumption, and autonomy among Thai women migrant workers. Hairong (2003, 588) suggests that where women were domesticated (i.e., brought into the house from agricultural work) as in post-Maoist China, wage work can be a means of escape from that domestication.

29. This had led some analysts (such as Tsing 2000a and Yanagisako 2002) to argue that Harvey and others who focus on flexible accumulation and its advantages for capitalists give agency only to capitalists and treat workers as passive. These critics miss the ways in which a focus on flexible accumulation can also take into account how workers creatively respond to flexibility. Additionally, they miss the fact that, in Harvey's approach, capitalists' agency in promoting flexibility and liberalization of trade is a response to earlier efforts by workers to improve their work conditions.

30. According to the World Bank, in the twenty years between 1975 and 1995, the number of people depending—directly or indirectly—on the sale of their labor power doubled to 2.5 billion (Panitch & Leys 2000, ix).

Chapter 7

1. See Tsing (2000a, 333) for a discussion of the "assumption of newness" and the neglect of earlier connections in much of the discussion of globalization. Similarly, Trouillot (2003, 48) writes about the "silencing of the past on a world scale."

2. See, e.g., Lloyd (1982, 99 and 118).

3. Sometimes this is explicit. Often it is implicit but evident in the neglect of class. See, e.g., Friedman (1994). According to Dominique Legros (1998, 394), Friedman describes young unemployed men who steal to consume, but he ignores their common identity in terms of lack of work.

4. For Trouillot, this emphasis on the market represents "the new master narrative of Western modernity" (2003, 48) pushed by marketing agents.

5. As Collins (2000) points out also, many flexible workers work in Fordist factories.

6. Although San Cosmeros/as are very aware of the possibility of movement to cheaper sites of production, this is not their only concern. They know also that their success is closely tied to the U.S. economy.

7. For a useful discussion of the subordination of Mexico's migration policy to U.S. interests, see Delgado Wise (2004).

8. I am grateful to June Nash for encouraging me to think about the implications of Wal-Mart's huge labor force.

9. See Cleveland, Iritani, & Marshall (2003) and Malkin (2004b) for more on such charges.

10. Multiple livelihoods are not unique to capitalism; peasant economies also rely on multiple ways to provide subsistence. But in peasant economies the majority of the benefits of labor do not feed into capital accumulation; i.e., wealth, not capital, characterizes the peasant economy.

11. For an important discussion of that growing inequality, see Blim (2004). Some commentators, especially writers in the popular press, have suggested that globalization has reduced inequality, not increased it. For an excellent discussion of how different ways of measuring inequality produce different conclusions, see Sutcliffe (2003).

12. For a recent example of such organization in Mexico, see Authers & Silver (2004).

13. See Mintz (1998) for a useful discussion of migration in the past; he provides an important reminder that we must not ignore history.

14. Not all movement was in the interests of capital. Struggles, for example, in southern Africa against colonialism attracted supporters from Cuba. Until the Soviet Union fell, there was a great deal of movement by workers for education and military support to and within the socialist countries.

15. This point is made very effectively by Appadurai in his article, "Disjuncture and Difference." Although he indicates the possibility of people now contesting the imaginaries of the "official mind" (1990, 7) and although he argues that the "the United States is no longer the puppeteer of a new world system of images" (1990, 4), he does not discuss the implications of this strikingly new interactive system for class and class struggle.

16. See, e.g., Herod (1997), Tsing (2000a), and Yanagisako (2002).

17. Tsing, like Inda & Rosaldo (2002, 6) and Gupta & Ferguson (2002, 68), reads Harvey as saying that flexible accumulation is a new stage (Tsing 2000b, 142). My reading of Harvey differs. I see his stress on uneven development as opening his analysis to a more heterogeneous global view. For example, in his discussion of flexible accumulation, he is careful to note its mixture with Fordism (1989, Ch. 11).

18. Trouillot (2003, 126) makes a similar point when he argues: "A multiple-site ethnography is quite reconcilable with an empiricist epistemology if it constructs the object of study as a mere multiplication of the places observed. The multiplication of localities does not solve the problem of their construction as given entities 'out there.'"

19. For a very interesting discussion of local views of cholera that show an appreciation of the links between localizing and globalizing processes and also an understanding of the role of transnational capital, see Briggs (2004).

20. See, e.g., Garcia Canclini (1992) and Inda & Rosaldo (2002).

21. This neglect corresponds to the point made by Sahlins (1976) about emic and etic views in his critique of materialist approaches. He argued that we fail to recognize that what Western anthropologists call an outsider (or etic) view is someone's (usually a Westerner's) insider (emic) view projected outside. Trouillot similarly takes such a view when he suggests that terms such as *modernity* and *development* are "North Atlantic universals . . . words that project the North Atlantic experience on a universal scale that they themselves have helped to create. North Atlantic universals are particulars that have gained a degree of universality . . ." (2003, 35).

22. It is important not to underestimate the power of the United States and of American capitalism. For an excellent discussion of that power, see Abu-Manneh's (2004) critical analysis of Michael Hardt & Antonio Negri's book, *Empire*.

23. As Blim points out, this approach to capitalism is not static; nor, as Yanagisako (2002, 186) notes, is it cultural. The household organization that discourages capital reinvestment in some economic contexts may, when the context changes, support rapid accumulation, or vice versa (Blim 1990, 256).

24. Polarski's (2003) use of the notion of insufficient skill ignores the ways in which labor is devalued despite its flexibilization, which often relies on workers having more skills to perform a variety of tasks.

25. For an interesting discussion of the growing autonomy and assertiveness among youth on a global scale because of their "simultaneous inclusion and exclusion" from neoliberal capitalism, see Comaroff & Comaroff (2000, 307).

26. As indicated in Chapter 5, it is important to note that the internal dynamics of that cooperation among kin are complex and varied. Reflecting broader patterns of inequality, gender and age are often important sources of strain and conflict under the surface of cooperation.

27. See, e.g., Mills (1999) and Ma (2001).

28. For an excellent analysis of how U.S. capitalism came to dominate and fuel discontent and opposition around the world, see Harvey (2003).

29. I disagree with Appadurai's assertion that imagination was "an elite pastime (thus not relevant to the lives of ordinary people)" (1990, 5) until the present. I think there is ample evidence of alternative imaginaries on the part of subordinate populations although, as Van Young (2001) recently pointed out regarding the ideology of indigenous groups in the Mexican struggle for independence, these imaginaries have often been neglected by researchers.

Bibliography

Abernathy, F., J. Dunlop, J. Hammond, and D. Weil. 2003. Globalization in the apparel and textile industries: What is new and what is not? In *Locating global advantage: Industry dynamics in a globalizing economy,* ed. R. Florida and M. Kenney. Palo Alto, CA: Stanford University Press.

Abu-Menneh, Bashir. 2004. The illusions of empire. *Monthly Review* 56 (2):1–12.

Alarcón González, Sandra. 2000. El tianguis global. In *Globalización: Una cuestión antropológica,* ed. Carmen Bueno Castellanos, 53–81. México City: Centro de Investigaciones y Estudios Superiores.

Alonso, Jose Antonio. 1984. The domestic clothing workers in the Mexican metropolis. In *Women and men and the international division of labor,* ed. M. P. Fernandez and June Nash. Albany, NY: SUNY Press.

———. 2000. Redes de subcontratación y globalización periférica en México. Paper presented at the annual meeting of the Southwest Council of Latin American Studies, Puebla, Mexico.

Anderson, Charles. 1968. Bankers as revolutionaries. In *The political economy of Mexico,* ed. C. Anderson and W. Glade, 103–196. Madison, WI: University of Wisconsin Press.

Appadurai, Arjun. 1990. Disjuncture and difference in the global cultural economy. *Public Culture* 2 (2):1–24.

———. 1996. *Modernity at large: Cultural dimensions of gobalization.* Minneapolis: University of Minnesota Press.

———. 1999. Globalization and the research imagination. *International Social Science Journal* 51 (160):229–238.

Arrighi, Giovanni. 1994. The long twentieth century: Money, power and the origins of our times. London: Verso.

Audely, John, Demetrios Papademetriou, Sandra Polaski, and Scott Vaughan. 2003. NAFTA's promise and reality: Lessons from Mexico for the hemisphere. *Carnegie Endowment Report,* November. http://www.ceip.org/NAFTA-REPORT (accessed June 20, 2004).

Authers, John. 2003. Walmex plans expansion as sales rise 10% retail. *The Financial Times,* July 15, 20.

Authers, John, and Sara Silver. 2004. Mexican workers sweat on labour ruling. *The Financial Times,* April 1, 8.

Babb, Florence. 2001. *After revolution: Mapping gender and cultural politics in neoliberal Nicaragua.* Austin, TX: University of Texas Press.

Bailey, Frederick. 1963. *Politics and social change: Orissa in 1959.* Berkeley, CA: University of California Press.

Bair, Jennifer, and Gary Gereffi. 2001. Local clusters in global chains: The causes and consequences of export dynamism in Torreon's blue jeans industry. *World Development* 29 (11):1885–1903.

Banamex, División de Estudios Económicos y Sociales. 1999. *Indicadores económicos y sociales,* Vol. LXXV, no. 879, March. Mexico, D.F.: Banco Nacional de México, Dept. of Economic Research.

Barkin, David. 1986. Mexico's albatross: The U.S. economy. In *Modern Mexico: State, economy and social conflict,* ed. Nora Hamilton and Timothy Harding, 106–127. Beverly Hills, CA: Sage.

Barnes, John. 1954. Class and committee in a Norwegian island parish. *Human Relations* 7:39–58.

Basch, Linda, Cristina Szanton Blanc, and Nina Glick Schiller. 1994. *Nations unbound: Transnational projects, postcolonial predicaments, and deterriorialized nation-states.* Langhorne, PA: Gordon & Breach.

Baudrillard, Jean. 1981. *For a critique of the political economy of the sign.* St. Louis: Telos.

———. 1995. On consumer society. In *Rethinking the subject: An anthology of contemporary European social thought,* ed. J. D. Fauqion, 193–204. Boulder, CO: Westview.

Becerril, Andrea. 1994. Cerraron más de 80% de empresas textiles en los dos últimos sexenios. *La Jornada* 6 (November):48.

Benería, Lourdes, and Shelley Feldman, eds. 1992. *Unequal burden: Economic crises, persistent poverty, and women's work.* Boulder, CO: Westview.

Benería, Lourdes, and Marta Roldan. 1987. *The crossroads of class and gender: Industrial homework, subcontracting, and household dynamics in Mexico City.* Chicago: University of Chicago Press.

Bernstein, Henry. 2001. The peasantry in global capitalism: Who, where and why? In *Socialist register 2001: Working classes, global realities,* ed. C. Leys and L. Panitch. London: Merlin.

Blim, Michael. 1990. *Made in Italy: Small-scale industrialization and its consequences.* New York: Praeger.

———. 1992. Introduction: The emerging global factory and anthropology. In *Anthropology and the global factory: Studies of the new industrialization in the late twentieth century,* ed. Michael Blim and Frances Rothstein, 1–32. New York: Bergin & Garvey.

———. 2000. Italian women after development: Employment, entrepreneurship, and domestic work in the third Italy. *International Journal of Family History* 6:257–270.

————. 2004. *Equality and economy: The global challenge.* Walnut Creek, CA: Alta Mira.

Bolles, A. Lynn. 1991. Surviving Manley and Seaga: Case studies of women's responses to structural adjustment policies. *Review of Radical Political Economics* 23 (3&4):20–36.

Bonacich, Edna, and Richard Appelbaum. 2000. *Behind the label: Inequality in the Los Angeles apparel industry.* Berkeley, CA: University of California Press.

Bourdieu, Pierre. 1984. *Distinction: A social critique of the judgement of taste.* Cambridge, MA: Harvard University Press.

Brecher, Jeremy, and Tim Costello. 1994. *Global village or global pillage: Economic reconstruction from the bottom up.* Boston: South End.

Brettell, Carolyn. 1986. *Men who migrate, women who wait: Population and history in a Portuguese parish.* Princeton, NJ: Princeton University Press.

Briggs, Charles. 2004. Theorizing modernity conspiratorially: Science, scale, and the political economy of public discourse in explanations of a cholera epidemic. *American Ethnologist* 31 (2):164–187.

Bruner, Edward. 1999. Return to Sumatra: 1957, 1997. *American Ethnologist* 26 (2):461–477.

Buechler, Hans C. and Judith-Maria Buechler. 1992. *Manufacturing against the odds: Small-scale producers in an Andean city.* Boulder, CO: Westview.

Burawoy, Michael. 2000. Introduction: Reaching for the global. In *Global ethnography: Forces, connections, and imaginations in a postmodern world,* ed. M. Burawoy, et al., 1–40. Berkeley, CA: University of California Press.

Campbell, Colin. 1995. The sociology of consumption. In *Acknowledging consumption,* ed. D. Miller, 96–126. London: Routledge.

Carrier, J. 1995. *Gifts and commodities: Exchange and western capitalism since 1700.* London: Routledge.

Carrier, J., and Josiah McC. Heyman. 1997. Consumption and political economy. *Journal of the Royal Anthropological Institute* 3 (2):353–373.

Castells, Manuel, and Alejandro Portes. 1989. World underneath: The origins, dynamics, and effects of the informal economy. In *The informal economy: Studies in advanced and less developed countries,* ed. L. Benton, M. Castells, and A. Portes. Baltimore: Johns Hopkins University Press.

Catalano, Ana Maria, and Marta Novick. 1995. Reconversión productivo y estrategias sindicales en Argentina: Renovación o ajuste táctico. In *Sindicalismo Latinoamericano: Entre la renovación y la resignación,* ed. Maria Silvia Portella de Castro and Achim Wachendorfer, 83–102. Caracas: Editorial Nueva Sociedad.

Chase-Dunn, Christopher, Yukio Kawano, and Benjamin Brewer. 2000. Trade globalization since 1795: Waves of integration in the world-system. *American Sociological Review* 65 (February):77–95.

Chavez M., Marcos. 1995. Sufre la manufactura su peor crisis de los últimos 15 años. *El Financiero,* April 24, 40.

Chen, Martha, Lesley O'Connell, and Jennefer Sebstad. 1999. Counting the invisible workforce: The case of homebased workers. *World Development* 27 (3):603–610.

Chin, Elizabeth. 2001. *Purchasing power: Black kids and American consumer culture.* Minneapolis: University of Minnesota Press.

Chinchilla, Norma, and Nora Hamilton. 1994. The garment industry and economic restructuring in Mexico and Central America. In *Global production: The apparel industry in the Pacific Rim,* ed. Edna Banocich, Lucie Cheng, Norma Chinchilla, Nora Hamilton, and Paul Ong, 287–308. Philadelphia: Temple University Press.

Clark, Kim. 1997. Apparel makers move south: The fallout from freer trade. *Fortune,* Nov. 24, 62.

Cleeland, Nancy, Evelyn Iritani, and Tyler Marshall. 2003. The Wal-Mart effect: Scouring the globe to give shoppers an $8.63 polo shirt. *Los Angeles Times,* Nov. 24, 1.

Cockcroft, James. 1990. *Mexico: Class formation, capital accumulation and the state.* New York: Monthly Review Press.

Collins, Jane. 2001. Flexible specialization and the garment industry. *Competition and Change* 5 (2):165–200.

———. 2002. Deterritorialization and workplace culture. *American Ethnologist* 29 (1):151–171.

———. 2003. *Threads: Gender, labor, and power in the global apparel industry.* Chicago: University of Chicago Press.

Comaroff, Jean, and John Comaroff. 1999. Occult economies and the violence of abstraction: Notes from the South African postcolony. *American Ethnologist* 26:279–301.

———. 2000. Millennial capitalism: First thoughts on a second coming. *Public Culture* 12 (2):291–343.

Cook, Maria Lorena. 1999. Trends in research on Latin American labor and industrial relations. *Latin American Research Review* 34 (1):237–254.

Cowie, Jefferson. 1999. *Capital moves: RCA's seventy-year quest for cheap labor.* Ithaca, NY: Cornell University Press.

Cruz, Angeles. 1994. Se duplicaron en cinco años microempresas. *La Jornada,* Oct. 24, 50, 60.

Cunningham, Hilary. 1999. The ethnography of transnational social activism: Understanding the global as local practice. *American Ethnologist* 26 (3):583–604.

Cypher, James. 1990. *State and capital in Mexico: Development policy since 1940.* Boulder, CO: Westview.

Darling, Juanita. 1992. Fears of free trade. *Los Angeles Times,* Nov. 9, sec. D.

Davis, Deborah. 2000. Introduction: A revolution in consumption. In *The consumer revolution in urban China,* ed. Deborah Davis, 1–24. Berkeley, CA: University of California Press.

De la Garza Toledo, Enrique. 1993. *Reestructuración productividad y respuesta sindical en México.* Mexico City: Instituto de Investigaciones Económicas.

Delgado Wise, Raúl. 2004. Labour and migration policies under Vicente Fox: Subordination to U.S. economic and geopolitical interests in Mexico. In *Transition: Neoliberal globalism, the state and civil society,* ed. Gerardo Otero, 138–153. London: Zed.

Dicken, Peter. 1998. *Global shift: Transforming the world economy.* New York: Guilford.

Dickerson, Kitty. 1995. *Textiles and apparel in the global economy.* Englewood Cliffs, NJ: Merrill.

Dinerman, Ina. 1978. Patterns of adaptation among households of U.S.-bound migrants from Michoacan, Mexico. *International Migration Review* 12 (4): 485–501.

Directorate-General of Budget, Accounting, and Statistics (DGBAS), and Council for Economic Planning and Development (CEPD). 1988. *Report on the manpower utilization survey in Taiwan area, Republic of China.* Taipei: DGBAS & CEPD.

Douglas, Mary, and Baron Isherwood. 1979. *The world of goods.* Boston: Basic.

Dow, James. 1977. Religion in the organization of a Mexican peasant economy. In *Peasant livelihood: Studies in economic anthropology and cultural ecology,* ed. James Dow and Rhoda Halperin, 215–226. New York: St. Martin's.

Dussel Peters, Enrique. 1998. Mexico's liberalization strategy, 10 years on: Results and alternatives. *Journal of Economic Issues* 32 (2):351–363.

Elson, Diane. 1994. Uneven development and the textiles and clothing industry. In *Capitalism and development,* ed. Leslie Sklair, 189–210.

Eraydin, Ayda, and Asuman Erendil. 1999. The role of female labour in industrial restructuring: New production processes and labour market relations in the Istanbul clothing industry. *Gender, Place and Culture: A Journal of Feminist Geography* 6 (3):259–273.

Escobar, Arturo. 1995. *Encountering development: The making and unmaking of the third world.* Princeton, NJ: Princeton University Press.

Escobar Latapi, Agustin, and Maria de la O. Martinez Castellanos. 1991. Small-scale industry and international migration in Guadalajara, Mexico. In *Migration, remittances and small business development,* ed. Sergio Diaz-Briquests and Sidney Weintraub. Boulder, CO: Westview.

Escobar Latapi, Agustin, and Bryan Roberts. 1991. Urban stratification, the middle classes, and economic change in Mexico. In *Social responses to Mexico's economic crisis of the 1980s,* ed. Mercedes Gonzalez de la Rocha and Agustin Escobar Latapi, 91–113. San Diego: Center for U.S.-Mexico Studies, University of California.

Felstead, Alan, and Nick Jewson. 1999. Flexible labour and non-standard employment: An agenda of issues. In *Global trends in flexible labour,* ed. A. Felstead and N. Jewson, 1–20. London: Macmillan.

Ferguson, James. 1999. *Expectations of modernity: Myths and meanings of urban life on the Zambian copperbelt.* Berkeley, CA: University of California Press.

Fernández-Kelly, Mária. 1983. *For we are sold, I and my people: Women and industry in Mexico's frontier.* Albany, NY: State University of New York Press.

Ferriss, Susan. 2003. Fox "weakened" in midterm Mexico elections. *The Atlanta Journal-Constitution,* July 8.

Frank, Andre Gunder. 1967. *Capitalism and underdevelopment in Latin America.* New York: Monthly Review Press.

Frankenberg, Ronald. 1957. *Village on the border: A social study of religion, politics and football in a North Wales community*. London: Cohen & West.

Freeman, Carla. 2000. *High tech and high heels in the global economy: Women, work, and pink-collar identities in the Caribbean*. Durham, NC: Duke University Press.

Friedman, Jonathan, ed. 1994b. The political economy of elegance: An African cult of beauty. In *Cultural identity and global process*, ed. Jonathan Friedman, 167–188. London: Sage.

Friedman, Thomas. 2004. What's that sound? *New York Times*, April 1.

Frobel, F., J. Heinrichs, and O. Kreye. 1981. *The new international division of labor*. London: Cambridge University Press.

Gale Group Inc. 2003. More potential than meets the eye. Dec. 8. http://80-web.lexis-nexis.com.researchport.umd.edu:2250/universe/printdoc (accessed June 3, 2004).

García, Brígida, and Orlandina de Oliveira. 1994. *Trabajo femenino y vida familiar en México*. Mexico City: El Colegio de México.

Garcia Canclini, Nestor. 1992. *Transforming modernity: Popular culture in Mexico*. Austin, TX: University of Texas Press.

———. 2001. *Consumers and citizens: Globalization and multicultural conflicts*, trans. G. Yudice. Minneapolis: University of Minnesota.

García Villanueva, Carlos, and Alfred Stoll. 1995. *Las relaciones laborales y su contexto económico y social*. In *Ruptura en las relaciones laborales*, ed. Manfred Wannoffel, 213–247. Mexico City: Fundación Friedrich Ebert and Nueva Sociedad.

Gereffi, Gary. 1994. The organization of buyer-driven commodity chains: How U.S. retailers shape overseas production networks. In *Commodity chains and global capitalism*, ed. G. Gereffi and M. Korzeniewicz, 95–122. Westport, CT: Greenwood.

———. 1997. The Mexico-U.S. Apparel Connection. In *Global restructuring, employment, and social inequality in urban Latin America*, ed. Rafael Larín and Richard Tardanico, 59–89. Coral Gables, FL: North-South Center Press.

Gibson, Charles. 1952. *Tlaxcala in the sixteenth century*. New Haven, CT: Yale University Press.

Gibson-Graham, J. K. 2000. Comment on Yang. *Current Anthropology* 41(4).

Giddens, Anthony. 1990. *The consequences of modernity*. Stanford, CA: Stanford University Press.

Gill, Lesley. 1999. *Teetering on the rim: Global restructuring, daily life, and the armed retreat of the Bolivian state*. New York: Columbia University Press.

Gledhill, John. 1999. Official masks and shadow powers: Toward an anthropology of the dark side of the state. *Urban Anthropology* 28 (3):199–251.

Glickman, Lawrence. 1997. *A living wage: American workers and the making of consumer society*. Ithaca, NY: Cornell University Press.

Gollás, Manuel, and Adalberto García Rocha. 1976. El desarrollo económico reciente de México. In *Contemporary Mexico*, ed. E. Monzon de Wilkie, M. Meyer, and J. Wilkie, 405–440. Berkeley, CA: University of California Press.

Gordon, David. 1988. The global economy: New edifice or crumbling foundations. *New Left Review* 168:24–64.

Green, Nancy. 1997. *Ready-to-wear and ready-to-work: A century of industry and immigrants in Paris and New York.* Durham, NC: Duke University Press.

Gupta, Akhil. 1998. *Postcolonial developments: Agriculture in the making of modern India.* Durham, NC: Duke University Press.

Gupta, Akhil, and James Ferguson. 2002. Beyond "culture": Space, identity, and the politics of difference. In *The anthropology of globalization: A reader,* ed. Jonathan Xavier Inda and Renato Rosaldo. Oxford: Blackwell.

Hairong, Yan. 2003. Spectralization of the rural: Reinterpreting the labor mobility of rural young women in post-Mao China. *American Ethnologist* 30 (4):578–596.

Hale, David. 2003. Mexico needs a Chinese shock. *The Financial Times,* July 9, 13.

Hanrath, Alexander. 2002. Wal-Mart hopes to clone its Mexican cash cow. *The Financial Times,* April 6, 15.

Hansen, Karen. 1997. *Keeping house in Lusaka.* New York: Columbia University Press.

———. 2000. *Salaula: The world of secondhand clothing and Zambia.* Chicago: University of Chicago Press

Hansen, Roger. 1971. *The politics of Mexican development.* Baltimore: Johns Hopkins University Press.

Hanson, Gordon. 1994. Industrial organization and U.S.-Mexico free trade: Evidence from the Mexican garment industry. In *Global production: The apparel industry in the Pacific Rim triangle,* ed. Edna Bonacich, Lucie Cheng, Norma Chinchilla, Nora Hamilton, and Paul Ong, 230–246. Philadelphia: Temple University Press.

Haraway, Donna. 1990. A manifesto for cyborgs and women: The reinvention of nature. In *Feminism/Postmodernism,* ed. L. Nicholson, 190–223. New York: Routledge.

Hardt, Michael, and Antonio Negri. 2000. *Empire.* Cambridge, MA: Harvard University Press.

Harvey, David. 1989. *The condition of postmodernity.* Cambridge, UK: Blackwell.

———. 1996. *Justice, nature and the geography of difference.* Cambridge, UK: Blackwell.

———. 2000. *Spaces of hope.* Berkeley, CA: University of California Press.

———. 2003. *The new imperialism.* London: Oxford University Press.

Hayward, Susana. 2004. Thousands protest Fox's address. *The Miami Herald,* Sept. 2, A11.

Held, David, David Goldblatt, Anthony McGrew, and Jonathan Perraton. *Global transformations: Politics, economics and culture.* Stanford, CA: Stanford University Press.

Hellman, Judith Adler. 1983. *Mexico in crisis.* New York: Holmes & Meier.

Herod, Andrew. 1997. From a geography of labor to a labor geography: Labor's spatial fix and the geography of capitalism. *Antipode* 29 (1):1–31.

Heyman McC., Josiah. 1991. *Life and labor on the border: Working people of northeastern Sonora, Mexico, 1886–1986*. Tucson, AZ: University of Arizona Press.

———. 1997. Imports and standards of justice on the Mexico-United States border. In *The allure of the foreign: Imported goods in postcolonial Latin America*, ed. Benjamin Orlove, 151–184. Ann Arbor, MI: University of Michigan Press.

Hite, Amy Bellone, and Jocelyn S. Viterna. 2005. Gendering class in Latin America: How women effect and experience change in the class structure. *Latin American Research Review* 40 (2):50–81.

Hoogvelt, Ankie. 1997. *The postcolonial world: The new political economy of development*. Baltimore: Johns Hopkins University Press.

Hsiung, Ping-Chun. 1996. *Living rooms as factories: Class, gender, and the satellite factory system in Taiwan*. Philadelphia: Temple University Press.

Inda, Jonathan Xavier, and Renato Rosaldo. 2002. Introduction: A world in motion. In *The anthropology of globalization: A reader*, ed. Jonathan Xavier Inda and Renato Rosaldo, 1–34. Oxford, UK: Blackwell.

Instituto Nacional de Estadística, Geografía e Informática (INEGI). 2001. *XII Censo General de Población y Vivienda 2000: Contar 2000*. Mexico City: Secretaría de Programación y Presupuesto.

Iritani, Evelyn, and R. Boudreaux. 2003. Mexico's factories shift gears to survive. *Los Angeles Times,* Jan. 5.

Jameson, Frederic. 1984. *Postmodernism, or the cultural logic of late capitalism*. Durham, NC: Duke University Press.

———. 1998. Notes on globalization as a philosophical issue. In *The cultures of globalization*, ed. F. Jameson and M. Miyoshi, 54–77. Durham, NC: Duke University Press.

Jarnow, Jeannette, and Kitty Dickerson. 1997. *Inside the fashion business*. Upper Saddle River, NJ: Prentice Hall.

Johnson, Allen. 2003. Chronicling cultures: Long-term field research in anthropology. *American Ethnologist* 30(4). http://www.aaanet.org/aes; accessed March 5, 2004.

Jones, Delmos. 1970. Towards a native anthropology. *Human Organization* 29 (4):251–259.

Jordan, Mary. 2003. Mexico now feels pinch of cheap labor: An economy built on low wages finds itself undercut by influx of Chinese imports. *The Washington Post,* Dec. 3, A19.

Kearney, Michael. 1995. The local and the global: The anthropology of globalization and transnationalism. *Annual Review of Anthropology* 24:547–565.

———. 1996. *Reconceptualizing the peasantry: Anthropology in global perspective*. Boulder, CO: Westview.

Keck, Margaret, and Kathryn Sikkink. 1998. Activists beyond borders. Ithaca, NY: Cornell University Press.

Kessler, Judi. 1999. The North American Free Trade Agreement, emerging apparel production networks and industrial upgrading: The Southern California/Mexico connection. *Review of International Political Economy* 6 (4):565–608.

Kilborn, Peter, and Lynnette Clemetson. 2002. Gains of 90s did not lift all, census shows. *New York Times,* June 5, A1, A24.

Kim, Seung-kyung. 1992. Women workers and the labor movement in South Korea. In *Anthropology and the global factory: Studies of the new industrialization in the late twentieth century,* ed. Michael Blim and Frances Rothstein, 220–237. New York: Bergin & Garvey.

Klein, Naomi. 1999. *No logo: Taking aim at the brand bullies.* New York: Picador.

Korzeniewicz, Roberto, and W. Smith. 2000. Poverty, inequality, and growth in Latin America: Searching for the high road to globalization. *Latin American Research Review* 35:7–54.

Kristof, Nicholas D. 2002. Let them sweat. *New York Times,* June 25, A25.

Kurtenbach, Elaine. 2003. Mexico touts benefits of free trade, urges others to yield on WTO issues. *The Associated Press,* Oct. 19. http://web.lexis-nexis.com.researchport.umd.edu:2250/universe/printdoc (accessed May 26, 2004).

Lash, Scott, and John Urry. 1987. *The end of organized capitalism.* Madison, WI: University of Wisconsin Press.

Lebowitz, Michael. 2004. What keeps capitalism going? *Monthly Review* 56 (2):19–23.

Lederman, Daniel, William Maloney, and Luis Serven. 2004. *Lessons from NAFTA for Latin America and the Caribbean: A summary of research findings.* Washington, DC: The World Bank.

Lee, Ching Kwan. 1998. *Gender and the South China miracle: Two worlds of factory women.* Berkeley, CA: University of California.

Lee, Eric. 1995. Workers unite. *Internet World,* August, 64–67.

Legros, Dominique. 1998. Review of Friedman's *Culture and Identity. Current Anthropology* 39 (3):394–395.

Lewis, Oscar. 1961. *The children of Sanchez.* New York: Random House.

Lins Ribeiro, Gustavo. 1998. Cybercultural politics: Political activism at a distance in a transnational world. In *Cultures of politics, politics of cultures,* ed. Sonia Alvarea, E. Dagnino, and A. Escobar, 26–352. Boulder, CO: Westview.

Lipietz, Alain. 1987. *Mirages and miracles: The crises of global Fordism.* London: Verso.

Lloyd, Peter. 1982. *A third world proletariat?* London: George Allen & Unwin.

Lui, Tai-lok, and Tony Man-yiu Chiu. 1999. Global restructuring and non-standard work in newly industrialised economies: The organisation of flexible production in Hong Kong and Taiwan. In Alan Felstead and Nick Jewson, eds. *Global Trends in Flexible Labour,* 166–180. London: Macmillan.

Lyons, John. 2003. Mexico seeing few advances: In first world race, nation falling behind. *Houston Chronicle,* Nov. 26.

Ma, Eric Kit-wai. 2001. Consuming satellite modernities. *Cultural Studies* 15 (3):444–463.

Malkin, Elisabeth. 2004a. Mexico's binational credit card. *New York Times,* June 16, W1.

———. 2004b. Mexican retailers unite against Wal-Mart. *New York Times,* July 9, W1, 7.

Mandel, Ernest. 1978. *Late capitalism*. London: Verso.

Marcus, George. 1998. *Ethnography through thick and thin*. Princeton, NJ: Princeton University Press.

Marx, Karl. 1978. The eighteenth brumaire of Louis Bonaparte. In *The Marx-Engels Reader*, ed. Robert Tucker. New York: W.W. Norton.

Mauss, Marcel. 1976. *The gift*. New York: W.W. Norton.

McMichael, Philip. 1996. *Development and social change: A global perspective*. Thousand Oaks, CA: Pine Forge.

Mies, Maria. 1982. *The lace makers of Narsapur: Indian housewives produce for the world market*. London: Zed.

Miller, Daniel. 1995a. Consumption and commodities. *Annual Review of Anthropology* 24:141–161.

———. 1995b. Consumption as the vanguard in history. In *Acknowledging consumption*, ed. D. Miller, 1–57. London: Routledge.

———. 1997. *Capitalism: An ethnographic account*. Oxford: Berg.

Mills, Mary Beth. 1999. *Thai women in the global labor force: Consuming desires, contested selves*. New Brunswick, NJ: Rutgers University Press.

Mintz, Sidney. 1985. *Sweetness and power*. New York: Viking.

———. 1998. The localization of anthropological practice: From area studies to transnationalism. *Critique of Anthropology* 18 (2):117–133.

Muñoz, Patricia, and Judith Calderon. 1997. Se encareció 8% la canasta básica en el primer trimestre. *La Jornada*, April 21, 16.

Nash, June. 1979. *We eat the mines and the mines eat us: Dependency and exploitation in Bolivian tin mines*. New York: Columbia University Press.

———. 1981. Ethnographic aspects of the world capitalist system. *Annual Review of Anthropology* 10:393–423.

———. 2001. *Mayan visions: The quest for autonomy in an age of globalization*. New York: Routledge.

Nash, June, and Maria Fernández-Kelly, eds. 1983. *Women, men and the international division of labor*. Albany, NY: State University of New York Press.

Navarette, Ifigenia Mode. 1960. *La distribución del ingreso y el desarrollo económico de México*. Mexico, D.F.: UNAM.

Niblo, Stephen. 1988. The impact of war: Mexico and World War II. Occasional paper no. 10. Melbourne: La Trobe University, Institute of Latin American Studies.

Nicholas, Ralph. 1965. Factions: A comparative analysis. In *Political systems and the distribution of power*, ed. M. Banton, 21–61. New York: Praeger.

Nutini, Hugo, and Betty Bell. 1984. *Ritual kinship: The structure and historical development of the compadrazgo system in rural Tlaxcala*. Pittsburgh: University of Pittsburgh Press.

O'Dougherty, Maureen. 2002. *Consumption intensified: The politics of middle-class daily life in Brazil*. Durham, NC: Duke University Press.

Ohmae, Kenichi. 1996. *The end of the nation state: The rise of regional economies*. London: HarperCollins.

Ong, Aihwa. 1987. *Spirits of resistance and capitalist discipline: Factory women in Malaysia*. Albany, NY: State University of New York Press.

Palmieri, Christopher, and Jose Aguayo. 1997. Good-bye, Gyandong, hello Jalisco. *Forbes* 159 (3):76–78.

Panitch, Leo, and Colin Leys. 2000. Preface. In *Socialist register 2001: Working classes, global realities,* ed. C. Leys and L. Panitch. London: Merlin.

Pedrero Nieto, Mercedes. 1990. Evolución de la participación económica femenina en los ochenta. *Revista Mexicana de Sociología* LII (1):133–149.

Phizacklea, Annie. 1988. Entrepreneurship, ethnicity and gender. In *Enterprising women: Ethnicity, economy and gender relations,* ed. Parminder Bhachu and Sallie Westwood. London: Routledge.

———. 1990. *Unpacking the fashion industry: Gender, racism, and class in production.* London: Routledge.

Piore, Michael. 1997. The economics of the sweatshop. In *No sweat: Fashion, fee trade, and the rights of garment workers,* ed. A. Ross. New York: Verso.

Piore, Michael and Charles Sabel. 1984. *The second industrial divide: Possibilities for prosperity.* New York: Basic.

Polarski, Sandra. 2003. Jobs, wages, and household income. In *NAFTA's promise and reality: Lessons from Mexico for the hemisphere,* ed. John Audely, Demetrios Papademetriou, Sandra Polaski, and Scott Vaughan, 11–24. Washington, DC: Carnegie International Endowment for Peace. http://www.ceip.org/NAFTA-REPORT (accessed June 20, 2004).

Portes, Alejandro, and Kelly Hoffman. 2003. Latin American class structures during the neoliberal era. *Latin American Research Review* 38 (1):40–82.

Pozas, María de los Angeles. 1993. *Industrial restructuring in Mexico: Corporate adaptation, technological innovation, and changing patterns of industrial relations in Monterrey.* La Jolla, CA: Center for U.S.-Mexican Studies, University of California, San Diego

Reuters. 2004. Walmex profit jumps 33 percent. *New York Times,* April 7.

Rivero Ríos, Miguel Angel, and Estela Suárez Aguilar. 1994. *Pequeña empresa y modernización: Análisis de dos dimensiones.* Cuernavaca, Morelos: UNAM Centro Regional de Investigaciones Multidisciplinarias.

Robertson, R. 1992. *Globalization.* London: Sage.

Rofel, Lisa. 1993. Rethinking modernity: Space and factory discipline in China. *Cultural Anthropology* 6 (1):93–114.

Rogers, Barbara. 1981. *The domestication of women: Discrimination in developing societies.* New York: St. Martin's.

Roseberry, William. 1988. Political economy. *Annual Review of Anthropology* 17:161–185.

———. 1989. *Anthropologies and history: Essays in culture, history and political economy.* New Brunswick, NJ: Rutgers University Press.

———. 1996. The rise of yuppie coffees and the reimagination of class in the United States. *American Anthropologist* 98 (4):762–775.

Rosenberg, Samuel, and June Lapidus. Contingent and non-standard work in the U.S. In *Global trends in flexible labour,* ed. A. Felstead and N. Jewson, 62–83. London: Macmillan.

Ross, Andrew. 1997. Introduction. In *No sweat: Fashion, free trade, and the rights of garment workers,* ed. A. Ross, 9–38. New York: Verso.

Ross, Robert, and Kent Trachte. 1990. *Global capitalism: The new leviathan.* Albany, NY: State University of New York Press.

Rostow, W. W. 1960. *The stages of economic growth. A non-communist manifesto.* Cambridge, NY: Cambridge University Press.

Rothstein. Frances. 1974. Factions in a rural community in Mexico. PhD diss., University of Pittsburgh.

———. 1979. The class basis of patron-client relations. *Latin American Perspectives* 6 (2):25–35.

———. 1982. *Three different worlds: Women, men and children in an industrializing community.* Westport, CT: Greenwood.

———. 1983. Women and men in the family economy: An analysis of the relations between the sexes in peasant communities. *Anthropological Quarterly* 56:10–23.

———. 1986. The new proletarians: Third world reality and first world categories. *Comparative Studies in Society and History* 28:217–238.

———. 1991. What happens to the past? Industrial migrants in Latin America. In *Anthropology and the global factory: Studies in the new industrialization of the late 20th century,* ed. Frances Rothstein and Michael Blim, 33–46. South Hadley, MA: Bersin & Garvey.

———. 1995. Gender and multiple income strategies in rural Mexico: A twenty-year perspective. In *Women in the Latin American development process,* ed. E. Acosta-Belen and C. Bose, 167–193. Philadelphia: Temple University Press.

———. 1996. Flexible accumulation, youth labor, and schooling in a rural community in Mexico. *Critique of Anthropology* 16:361–380.

———. 1999. Declining odds: Kinship, women's employment and political economy in rural Mexico. *American Anthropologist* 101(3).

———. 2000. Flexible work and post-modern culture: The impact of globalization on work and culture in rural Mexico. *Anthropology of Work Review* 11 (1):3–7.

———. 2005a. Flexibility for whom? Small-scale garment manufacturing in rural Mexico. In *Petty capitalists and globalization: Flexibility, entrepreneurship, and economic development,* ed. Alan Smart and Josephine Smart, 67–82. Alba·1y, NY: SUNY Press.

———. 2005b. Challenging consumption theory: Production and consumption in central Mexico. *Critique of Anthropology* 25 (3):279–306.

Rouse, Roger. 1991. Mexican migration and the social space of postmodernism. *Diaspora* 1 (1):8–23.

Rozhon, Tracie. 2003. Decision seen soon on maker of Calvin Klein women's line. *New York Times,* June 18, C1, C18.

Rubinstein, Hymie. 1983. Remittances and rural underdevelopment in the English-speaking Caribbean. *Human Organization* 2 (4):295–306.

Safa, Helen. 1981. Runaway shops and female employment: The search for cheap labor. *Signs* 7 (2):418–433.

———. 1995. *The myth of the male breadwinner: Women and industrialization in the Caribbean.* Boulder, CO: Westview.

Sahlins, Marshall. 1976. *Culture and practical reason.* Chicago: University of Chicago.

Schneider, Jane. 1994. In and out of polyester: Desire, disdain and global fiber competitions. *Anthropology Today* 19 (4):2–9.

Secretaría de Desarrollo Económico (SEDECO). 2000. *Directorio industrial:*

Empresas por corredor industrial. Tlaxcala, Mexico: Gobierno del Estado de Tlaxcala.

Sheahan, John. 1997. Effects of liberalization programs on poverty and inequality: Chile, Mexico, and Peru. *Latin American Research Review* 32 (3):7–37.

Simmons, Colin, and Christos Kalantaridis. 1994. Flexible specialiazation in the southern Europe periphery: The growth of garment manufacturing in Poenia County, Greece. *Comparative Studies in Society and History* 36: 200–223.

———. 1996. Entrepreneurial strategies in southern Europe: Rural workers in the garment industry in Greece. *Journal of Economic Issues* 30:121–143.

Smart, Alan and Josephine Smart, eds. 2005. *Petty capitalists and globalization: Flexibility, entrepreneurship and economic development.* Albany, NY: SUNY Press.

Smith, Neil. 1997. The satanic geographies of globalization: Uneven development in the 1990s. *Public Culture* 10 (1):169–189.

Sparr, Pamela, ed. 1994. *Mortgaging women's lives: Feminist critiques of structural adjustment.* London: Zed.

Standing, Guy. 1999. Global feminization through flexible labor: A theme revisited. *World Development* 27 (3):583–602.

Stephen, Lynn. 1991. *Zapotec women.* Austin, TX: University of Texas Press.

Stevenson, Mark. 2003. In Mexico, trade war with China being tough with vendors, 'Buy Mexican' ad campaigns. *The Associated Press,* Nov. 23. http://web.lexis-nexis.com/universe/document? (accessed Nov. 24, 2004).

Steward, Julian. 1955. *Theory of culture change.* Urbana, IL: University of Illinois Press.

Stiglitz, Joseph. 2002. *Globalization and its discontents.* New York: Norton.

———. 2004. The broken promise of NAFTA. *New York Times,* Jan. 6, A23.

Stinchcombe, Arthur. 1987. Flexible specialization. *Sociological Forum* 1 (2): 185–190.

Storper, Michael. 2000. Lived effects of the contemporary economy: Globalization, inequality, and consumer society. *Public Culture* 12 (12):375–409.

Suárez Aguilar, Estela. 1994. *La pequeña empresa en el proceso de modernización industrial y tecnológica en México. La parte: La pequeña y mediana en la industria del vestido.* Cuernavaca, Morelos: UNAM Centro Regional de Investigaciones Multidisciplinarias.

Susser, Ida. 1982. *Norman Street: Poverty and politics in an urban neighborhood.* New York: Oxford.

———. 1992. Women as political actors in rural Puerto Rico: continuity and change. In *Anthropology and the global factory: Studies of the new industrialization in the late twentieth century,* ed. Michael Blim and Frances Rothstein, 206–219. New York: Bergin & Garvey.

Sutcliffe, Bob. 2003. A more or less unequal world: World income distribution in the twentieth century. *Indicators* 2 (3):24–70.

Tanski, Janet, and Dan French. 2001. Capital concentration and market power in Mexico's manufacturing industry: Has trade liberalization made a difference? *Journal of Economic Issues* 35 (3):675–712.

Taplin, Ian. 1996. Rethinking flexibility: The case of the apparel industry. *Review of Social Economy* 54:191–221.

Tardanico, Richard, and Rafael Menjívar Larín, eds. 1997. *Global restructuring, employment, and social inequality in urban Latin America.* Coral Gables, FL: North-South Center Press, University of Miami.

Tokman, Victor E., and Emilio Klein, Eds. 1996. *Regulation and the informal economy: Microenterprises in Chile, Ecuador, and Jamaica.* Cambridge, UK: Cambridge University Press.

Trouillot, Michel-Rolph. 2003. *Global transformations: Anthropology and the modern world.* New York: Palgrave Macmillan.

Tsing, Anna. 2000a. The global situation. *Cultural Anthropology* 15 (3): 327–361.

———. 2000b. The economy of appearances. *Public Culture* 12 (1):115–144.

Tuñón Pablos, Julia. 1999. *Women in Mexico: A past unveiled.* Austin, TX: University of Texas Press.

Urrutia, Alonso, Mireya Cuellar, and Fabiola Martinx. 2003. El conteo rápido del IFE da al PRI 34.4 por ciento de la votación nacional. *La Jornada,* July 7.

U.S. Department of Commerce. International Trade Commission, Office of Textiles and Apparel. May 1998. *Major shippers report: Section one: Textiles and apparel imports by category.* http://otexa.ita.doc.gov/msr/carvo.htm (accessed May 30, 1998).

———. June 2003. *Major shippers report: Section one: Textiles and apparel imports by category.* http://otexa.ita.doc.gov/msr/carvo.htm (accessed June 10, 2003).

———. June 2005. *Major shippers report by country.* http://otexa.ita.doc.gov/msr/carcty/a2010.htm (accessed June 9, 2005).

U.S. Department of State. Bureau of Economic and Business Affairs. February 2002. *2001 country reports on economic policy.* http://www.state.gov/e/eb/rls/rpts/eptp (accessed May 27, 2002).

Van Young, Eric. 2001. *The other rebellion: Popular violence, ideology, and the Mexican struggle for independence.* Stanford, CA: Stanford University Press.

Velasco Contreras, Elizabeth. 2001. En marcha, el programa para el fortalecimiento de la economía. *La Jornada,* Oct. 2, 30.

Waldinger, Roger. 1986. *Through the eye of the needle: Immigrants and enterprise in New York's garment trades.* New York: New York University Press.

Weiner, Tim. 2003. Wal-Mart invades and Mexico gladly surrenders. *New York Times,* Dec. 6.

———. 2003. Free trade accord at age 10: The growing pains are clear. *New York Times,* Dec. 27, A1, A8.

White, Leslie. 1959. *The Evolution of culture.* New York: McGraw-Hill.

Williamson, John. 2000. What should the World Bank think about the Washington Consensus? *The World Bank Research Observer* 15 (2):251–264.

Wilson, Fiona. 1999. Gendered histories: Garment production and migration in Mexico. *Environment and Planning* 31 (2):327–343.

Wilson, Patricia. 1992. *Exports and local development: Mexico's new maquiladoras.* Austin, TX: University of Texas Press.

Wilson, Tamar Diana. 1998. Approaches to uderstanding the position of women workers in the informal sector. *Latin American Perspectives* 25 (2):105–119.

Wionczek, Miguel. 1974. *La inversión extranjera privada: Problemas y perspectivas.* In *La sociedad Mexicana: Presente y futuro,* ed. Miguel Wionczek. Mexico, D.F.: Fondo de Cultura Económica.

Wolf, Eric. 1956. Aspects of group relations in a complex society. *American Anthropologist* 58:1065–1078.

———. 1982. *Europe and the people without history.* Berkeley, CA: University of California Press.

———. 1986. The vicissitudes of the closed corporate peasant community. *American Ethnologist* 13:325–329.

Yanigasako, Sylvia. 2002. *Producing culture and capital: Family firms in Italy.* Princeton, NJ: Princeton University Press.

Ypeig, Annelou. 2000. *Producing against poverty: Female and male micro-entrepreneurs in Lima, Peru.* Amsterdam: Amsterdam University Press.

Zúñiga, David. 2000. 90% de trabajadores del país ganan menos de cinco minisalarios. *La Jornada,* Oct. 12.

———. 2003. Empresas nacionales, practicamente excluídas del comercio internacional. *La Jornada,* July 28.

Index

peasant-workers, 144–145
Piore, Michael, 64–66, 72
postcolonial condition, 129
post-fordism, 9, 12, 113
poverty, 35, 162n12
proletariat. *See* working class
Puebla (city), 40, 121
Puebla (state), 37, 40, 115–116; factory work in, 16, 17, 24, 29; travel to, 51

resistance, 11, 18, 32, 137, 144; diverse forms of, 151–152
ritual kinship, 51–52, 85

Sabel, Charles, 64–66, 72
San Cosme Mazatecochco, 1–3, **2**, 6–10; capitalism in, 156–157; class in, 132–136; commodity consumption in, 115, 116, 118–128; community development, 16, 56–57; economic crisis in, 17, 18, 29–30; economic miracle in, 27–30; effects of neoliberalism, 36–37, 60, 158–159; fieldwork in, 14–15, 16, 141–142; garment production in, 10, 18, 20; identities in, 119–120, 129–130; Internet service in, 141, **142;** kinship in, 11, 12; land in, 24; men of, 10, 11, 16; migration from, 10, 11, 17, 23, 151, 152, 160; occupations of women and men in, **100**; outsiders in, 40; relations beyond the community, 19–20; small-scale agriculture in, 28, 29; unions in, 146; wage labor, 11, 16; women, 11
San Francisco Papalotla, 28, 29, 44, 129; dominance of, 50; *maquiladoras* in, 99; ritual kin in, 51
state: changing role of, 33–34, 35; encouraging capital accumulation, 133, 145; policies of, 10, 24–28, 32, 34
Stephen, Lynn, 126

Steward, Julian, 6
structural adjustment, 17, 112–113, 114, 162n18, 168n5
subsistence cultivation, 18, 24, 107; during economic crisis, 60–61
sweatshops, 104, 161n1

textile industry, 16
time-space compression, 7–8, 105
Tlaxcala (city), 14, 15, 16; travel to, 51
Tlaxcala (state), 14, 24, 27, 28, 37, 40, 41; development program, 57; *maquiladoras* in, 163n16
trade liberalization. *See* free trade
transnational advocacy networks, 152
Tsing, Anna, 154–155, 161n3, 169n29, 169n1, 170n16

unions, 16, 56, 134; controlled by the state, 135; independent, 151, 170n12; in San Cosme, 146
United States, 25, 26, 30–31, 36, 40, 41, 78, 147, 163n15; migration to, 93, 138
Urry, John, 84

wage labor, 3, 6, 16, 150; naturalness of, 157. *See also* factory work
wages, 81, 82, 165n8, 165n9
Wal-Mart, 105, 106, 148, 170n9
Washington Consensus, the, 3, 31
White, Lesley, 6
Wolf, Eric, 5, 6, 7, 23
women: and consumption, 126; dependence on men, 95; domestication of, 94–95; employment of, 37, 82; effect of men's factory work on, 53–56; exclusion from factory work, 94; as family labor, 89; Federal Labor Law against, 95; flexibility and, 66; increased labor force participation and self-employment, 61–62, 96, **97**; opportunities for, 94–95, 98–102; workshop ownership, 81, 82